I dedicate this book to you, the positive thinkers, the positive outlookers of life, and to those who possess the power of positivity and believe that anything can be achieved if you put your mind to it.

ANT MIDDLETON

ZERO NEGATIVITY

THE POWER OF POSITIVE THINKING

HarperCollins*Publishers*

BY THE SAME AUTHOR

First Man In
The Fear Bubble

HarperCollins*Publishers*
1 London Bridge Street
London SE1 9GF

www.harpercollins.co.uk

First published by HarperCollins*Publishers* 2020

1 3 5 7 9 10 8 6 4 2

© Anthony Middleton 2020

Anthony Middleton asserts the moral right to
be identified as the author of this work

A catalogue record of this book is
available from the British Library

HB ISBN 978-0-00-833651-6
PB ISBN 978-0-00-833652-3

Printed and bound in Great Britain by
CPI Group (UK) Ltd, Croydon

MIX
Paper from
responsible sources
FSC™ C007454

This book is produced from independently certified FSC™ paper
to ensure responsible forest management.

For more information visit: www.harpercollins.co.uk/green

CONTENTS

CONTENTS

INTRODUCTION

BULLETPROOF

IT COULD BE any night. We could be anywhere.

This one starts in a huge encampment out in the grim, grey, enemy-crawling desert. It's stuffed with millions upon millions of dollars of the most advanced military equipment known to man. During the day, hundreds of US personnel hurry about with their sleeves rolled up, their berets set just so and their regulation assault rifles slung over their shoulders. CIA operatives in tan chinos and sporting Oakley shades do their best to pretend they don't exist. All around us are massive hangars housing fully kitted-out Hawks, Apaches and Chinooks. This isn't a massive surprise. The gyms here are bigger than an entire British base.

There's an almost hallucinogenic difference between the US camp and my destination later tonight, a shabby, run-down compound deep in the desert. It's difficult to believe they exist in the same world, let alone the same country. For now, though, they're both shrouded by darkness, at that time when everything changes and objects lose the reassuring form they possessed in the day: the shadow cast by a dog is easily mistaken for a whole patrol of men, a dislodged stone sounds like a rifle shot.

We learned where we were going at a briefing two hours ago, and the following minutes have passed quickly. I'm absorbed by routines that have become deeply familiar to me. I check my kit, again and again and again. I know that if I make just one slip – a piece of carelessness in cleaning my weapon, an oversight when packing ammunition – I might as well be writing my own death sentence. I don't want my last thoughts on this planet to begin, 'If only …'

Once I'm sorted, I enter the coordinates of our target into my GPS. I check the map, looking for reference points. If I see a mountain, for instance, I'll want to remember its location so that when I see its triple peaks out of the corner of my right eye in the dark, I'll know we're heading in the right direction. After that, I look hard at every piece of intelligence that's come my way and stare at the buildings I'll soon be storming into. I commit every detail to memory, so I won't be surprised by a corridor that opens out unexpectedly or a door that leads nowhere.

I always have the same questions running through my head. What is my job? Where do I go first? Where can I expect to find armed guards? Are there civilians? When I see the target, how will I identify him? I try to break every element down until I've reached a point where I understand it completely. I have a visual mind. When I'm looking at a map there will come a moment when its contours levitate into three dimensions above the page.

When I've done all this, I run through the first plan, and for each key moment try to find an alternative in case something goes wrong. If this door won't open, how else will we get in? Do we blow it off its hinges? Try an entrance round the back? It's another form of visualisation. I try to imagine every single eventuality to the point where I almost have a muscle memory of it. When the action actually does unfold, it will be as if I've already experienced it.

The skill is not to overthink it or to overload yourself with more information than necessary. You need to stay nimble; you've got to be able to think on your feet. If you've absorbed too many details, your thinking will be rigid, undynamic. As Mike Tyson once said: 'Everybody has a plan until they get punched in the mouth.' When the shit hits the fan – as it inevitably will at some point – I know that I still have the foundations of the mission in my head. Everything else can be supplied by my training.

THE FIRST FEW times I went into combat I had a nervous feeling in the pit of my stomach that ended up destroying my appetite. It didn't last long. I don't stuff my face before setting out, but I have to make sure I'm fed and watered. Carbed up. The mission could last two or three hours. It could also unfold over two or three days.

Some people seek out others. I just want to be by myself and try to grab as much time alone as I can. I want to get into the zone, run the mission through my head again. Tonight I'm calm. This hasn't always been the way. There have been occasions when I was able to actually *see* my nerves. One night, before a mission that had very particular personal resonance for me, I remember how the adrenaline came on like a king tide. I could feel it in my veins, surging and throbbing in great liquid waves. I'd headed over to the hangar ahead of my comrades half an hour early, to give myself the chance to have a brew in the silence before it all kicked off. But as I dipped my spoon into the packet of sugar, I noticed it was shaking. Little granules were falling off its sides and back into the packet. I watched for a moment, focused on each crystal as it tumbled downwards, then looked up anxiously toward the hangar door. This was no good. I had to get myself under control.

I tried forcing myself to steady my breathing, slowing it down, deepening my draws of oxygen. But when I looked down, the spoon was still shaking. At that moment I heard footsteps. I glanced up. It was another soldier. Give it thirty seconds and there wouldn't be any sugar left on the fucking thing. The other guy's footsteps came closer towards me, echoing in the vast, dark hangar. As he approached, I felt a sudden rage at my weakness. It blasted through me, but I managed to control it. I allowed the fury to fill me up, every limb now engorged and primed, every muscle taut. A few years earlier, my anger would have taken over. Now I'd learned to use it like an injection of insanely powerful steroids. I was ten times stronger than I'd been a moment ago. A hundred times stronger. I looked at the spoon. It was almost still.

'Making a brew?' he asked.

'Yes, mate,' I said, looking up with a calm smile. 'Have we got any biscuits?'

I know that controlling my emotions is so important. I have no problem showing how I feel to others – I don't mind them knowing that I'm human and that I'm vulnerable – but in some situations it's selfish to unsettle others by exposing the worst of yourself. So whatever I'm thinking inside, I work hard to make sure nobody can guess that I'm anything other than relaxed and ready.

I SPEND A few more minutes alone in the hangar. Even now, at the beginning of a night that I know could well be my last, it's strange to be confronted by scenes that speak so strongly of another, more mundane kind of existence. It's also oddly reassuring, a reminder that no matter what happens later, life will go on without me.

Take the table in the corner. It's a sight that in all the years I've served in the forces I've somehow never been able to escape. Everywhere I go, it's exactly like this – an arrangement as British as the royal wave. The shitty table with the foldaway legs and the shiny brown wood-effect surface. The chipped mug full of spoons with the faded writing on it: HAPPY BIRTHDAY DAD or MG HOLDINGS LTD. The steel urn with the red light and the black power cord and the old taped-on Biro notice that warns 'CARE! HOT!', the trusty half-empty box of PG Tips, next to it the scaggy jar of Nescafe with the cracked lid. And, last but not least, the damp-stained, crumpled packet of Tate & Lyle, the sugar inside it rocky and discoloured after being dipped in by too many wet spoons. In many ways it's depressing, but there's something about this collection of tatty objects that never fails to make me smile.

After a while I'm joined by the rest of the team and we head out onto the night-shrouded pan. The silhouette of the Chinook is hard to make out at first, then slowly it comes into focus. Even standing idle, it projects brute power. With its rotors extended, it's a big, ugly beast: thirty metres long, almost six metres tall, and with two M134 7.62mm Miniguns and two M240 7.62mm belt-fed machine guns bristling menacingly on either side. The helicopter has been stripped of all excess weight to aid manoeuvrability, its walls taken right back to the outer panels. Ungainly as it is, I feel a strange affection for the vehicle that has come to play such a big part in my life. More than the operations themselves, it's the minutes, hours even, that we spend in this machine that I remember most clearly. So much of what happens in combat is instinctive, with events often being over almost before they've begun. But here in the Chinook there's always time for me to think and reflect.

After we clamber aboard we all sit there in our team locations – our positions dictated by how we'll deploy as soon as we step off the aircraft. We sit evenly spaced on benches that run parallel to the helicopter's sides. It's more comfortable than you might think. Then the engine starts. You hear a loud, piercing noise, a wail so loud that for a moment it's almost unbearable, before it gives way to the heavy whirring of the rotors. I feel a tiny pulse of exhilaration as they pick up speed. Here we go again, I think. Then the Chinook's hatch door rises and we're lifted into the night air.

Whoomp whoomp whoomp.

Back at the base we were joking around, taking photos and laughing; far more relaxed, far more chilled out than you'd expect. We all know what we're doing, we know what we're capable of, so it creates a playfulness that often expresses itself in extremely bleak humour.

That mood is over now. The helicopter climbing up is the sign for me: shit's happening now, we're not turning back. I'm getting into the zone. I look around at the other men. They look back. Nobody says anything, but we exchange glances. Are we all here? Are we all good? Are we all ready?

Whoomp whoomp whoomp.

Moments pass, and when I next look up I see everyone lost in their own little zones, psyching themselves up. Some just stare into the middle distance, others have their iPods on. It's a night mission, so the uncanniness of our environment is heightened by the fact that, inside and out, we're flying without lights in order to try to avoid unwanted attention. Looking out the window, I can see the dark silhouettes of the mountains that we're flying between, keeping as low – and as low key – as possible. I try to match them to the topography I'd seen on the map earlier in the evening. It's reassuring to have even a vague idea of where we are amid the all-consuming darkness.

Whoomp whoomp whoomp.

The rotors sound distant to me now, almost obliterated by the raw aggression pulsing through my headphones. It's cold at night. I'm swaddled in a big fucking jacket. It's XXXL, more duvet than coat. I listen to heavy metal – Slipknot, Metallica, Rage Against the Machine – at full volume. Drums crashing, guitars distorted and dirty, voices screaming. Wave upon wave of nasty, violent music that sends my heart racing, makes every nerve in my body feel alive.

Whoomp whoomp whoomp.

Forty minutes into the flight, a voice in my earpiece. It's the sergeant major: 'Ten-minute call.' My heart begins to thud. I put on my helmet, connect my night-vision goggles (NVGs) and begin getting used to seeing with them. They send me into a narrow, grainy world of green and black. When I first started to wear them they made me feel a bit like I was drunk, reeling about because my depth perception was way off and everything was tinged with a nauseous green fog. Now I can see as clearly with them as with my naked eyes. Once I get out there I know I'll be able to judge every crack in a door, every barely visible movement on the other side of a dark room, with incredible accuracy. My enemies will be struggling in the dark; I'll be able to see things down to the nearest millimetre.

Whoomp whoomp whoomp.

Only the briefest stretch of time separates us from the moment when we'll have to burst out of the helicopter and into the dust cloud it always kicks up as it lands. I've done it many times over, but the experience never fails to get my adrenaline surging. It's when we know we're at our most vulnerable. Eight to ten seconds when your world is reduced to a beige haze and the knowledge that every extra moment spent in it is an extra moment of danger. Propelled by the Chinook's downdraft you have to sprint, breath hoarse in your chest, legs burning with a sudden rush of lactic acid. You're not thinking of anything except escaping the dust cloud.

You're hyper-alert. It's almost like you don't miss a thing, as if all of your senses have been supercharged. You have to be able to absorb and assess every piece of information that's thrown at you, and you've got to do it in fractions of seconds.

And yet there's something euphoric about that time. People always say to me: Ant, you're an adrenaline junkie.

They're wrong. I'm very calculated. I'm in control. I'm not a reckless person. But what I've realised is that there will always be part of me that's in love with walking that delicate line that separates life and death. I'm most alive during those beautiful, uncomplicated fragments of time when all the noise and mess falls away and your existence is stripped back to two stark outcomes. You're either going to live, or you're going to die. That's it. It's the purest form of life: to me, the ultimate form of peace. You run like fuck to reach the other side; and then you're through, ready to slide into a gun position.

Whoomp whoomp whoomp.

More time passes. I know how easy it would be to drift into a negative spiral. One thought leads to another. Before you know it, you're crippled, your head filled with doubt. You've ceased to live in the here and now and have instead stepped into a world of what ifs and maybes. I know that lots of people suffer from imposter syndrome. I don't. I'm here, in this helicopter, *because* I'm good at my job. If I start wondering whether I deserve it, if I let doubts creep in, I'll inhibit my ability to do what I do effectively. You don't want to be that guy who loses his nerve and pokes his head around the corner, in the process making himself the world's easiest target. As far as I'm concerned, when I hit the ground, I'm the best soldier in the world.

The first time I came under fire, all that ran through my head afterwards, when the mission was over, was: *That's it, that's it done.* I'd held my nerve, I didn't fall apart. Now it's become part of my everyday existence, although being shot at during the night will always remain strange to me. You don't see the bullets, or where they're coming from. But you hear the whipcrack as they zip past you. The louder the snap, the nearer the miss. As time goes by you learn to tell the different weapons apart. That's an AK-47; that's a heavy machine gun. Fuck, an RPG.

I don't let it affect me. I think to myself, if I do get hit then hopefully it'll be in the head and I won't know a fucking thing about it. If it's another part of my body, then I'll deal with it there and then. Worrying won't make me any safer. Far better to focus on the way I move, the way I use the cover. I'm fast, confident and aggressive. I believe I can do things that the majority of other people can't. Positive thinking. If I fixate on the bullets, I'll stop or I'll hide, and probably end up in more danger. I never go out there thinking I'll be shot. I've always believed I'll be getting back on that helicopter on the way home.

I'm sure the enemy can see my aggression. I'm sure too that it gets into their heads. If your enemy *looks* bulletproof, then the chances are that part of you might begin to believe they really are.

Whoomp whoomp whoomp.

The sergeant major signals the five-minute call. I switch into another zone. My hands run across all of my webbing and equipment. Checking. Checking again. Checking again.

I'm still cool, still thinking calmly about what's ahead of us. Is my weapon's magazine in securely. Is it cocked? Do I have a round in the chamber? Safety catch is on.

My weapons feel as much part of my body as my hands or knees. There's something I can't fully explain to anyone else about the way I hold and nurture them. I've moulded my rifle with little bits of tape on its stock so that it fits perfectly into my arms; so perfectly that I can operate it with one hand. Once I go into combat I know exactly where it is at every moment. When I move, it moves. It never feels as if there's any conscious effort. Lifting my rifle is, to me, no different to stretching out a leg. I can carry it through tight spaces – narrow doors, tiny cubbyholes – without it ever snagging or catching on anything. It's my life. It's everything.

Two-minute call.

Whoomp whoomp whoomp.

I can feel the Chinook losing height, the sensation of rapid but controlled falling in the core of my body merging uncomfortably with my rising adrenaline. We all stand up, face the door and stabilise ourselves for landing by placing our hands shoulder to shoulder.

My mind flicks forward again, imagining those seconds before I kick the first door down. I don't fuck around; I don't overthink. I just commit. I know I have to get through it, no matter what. Holding back won't help me. What you're unbelievably conscious of in those seconds is the people around you. You're stacked up against the doorframe, about to launch yourself into a life-or-death situation, your two comrades sweeping to the other side of the entrance. You're all looking after each other. You need to know, with absolute, unshakeable confidence, that whatever happens to you, they'll get the job done, or take a bullet for you. These are men you've trained with, kicked doors down with. You know how they operate. The look doesn't last long. I nod, or squeeze a shoulder. *Let's fucking do this.*

A lot of the doors are shitty, worm-eaten relics. One kick and they smash almost into dust; you feel like Superman. Others you have to hammer away at – the tension rising with every blow that doesn't knock it over. But sometimes on those missions where everything is about discretion, once you get flowing you don't even need to kick them open. Keep it simple. If the door's already unlocked, then it probably doesn't need your size tens being put through it. There's you and another guy, lined up on the wall either side, whispering over our radio. 'Try the door.' The look … then, 'One, two, three.' Boom. You're through, your men behind you.

Whoomp whoomp whoomp.

I slip the jacket off, remove my headphones and get down on one knee. Another silent check of all the lads. Seeing them fills me with confidence. They're good guys. I know I can rely on them. I *have* to rely on them. I'm in that fucking zone. *Whoomp whoomp whoomp.* My NVGs are down over my eyes. The helicopter surges down to hit the ground, making my stomach feel as if it's trying to swallow my heart. No matter how many times I've been in this position, I've never quite got used to the speed with which these massive twin-rotored machines can be made to move. It's truly incredible. Their pilots hurl them around mid-air like they're plastic toys. If they see an RPG coming towards them, they can spin them on a dime, dancing elegantly out of its path.

Ready. Ready. Ready. Waiting for the tailgate to go down. A mechanical whirr, and the world outside comes steadily into view. The cold, dry, woody air of the desert rushes in, along with great billows of dust. We launch ourselves straight out.

GO.

ALL OF THIS feels like a long time ago. When I think about that part of my life, it sometimes seems as if all of these things were experienced by a completely different man. So much has happened since. I am no longer a warrior; I'm a TV presenter, an author and a businessman. I've experienced crushing lows, and incredible highs. I've been to prison, the top of Mount Everest, to places I'd never previously have believed possible. But there's a thread that connects that version of me to the one currently writing this book: positivity.

Although I didn't necessarily realise it back then, it was thinking positively that helped me to thrive in the armed forces. It was thinking positively that meant I could go into combat feeling as if I were bulletproof. And it's been the same ever since. My positive mentality has enabled me to overcome setbacks that might otherwise have been fatal; and it has allowed me to seize opportunities that another person might have let slip through their hands.

I was born positive. Maybe it was something I inherited from my father or absorbed from him in the short time I was with him on the planet. But my mindset is also the result of the way my life has unfolded. Don't get me wrong – it's been a long, tough process. The growth of my positivity has been mirrored by the ways in which I've grown as a man. The missteps I've taken have been just as significant as the moments when I've looked to be flying. I wasn't the finished article when I was in the Special Forces, and I'm far from the finished article now, but I know I can look back at key moments in my life and tell myself that I've drawn the right lessons from them. I'm not sure I'd have been able to attain this knowledge had I not been through trials and tribulations, shit moments and low days, setbacks and outright failures.

Usually in this kind of book the author will tell you that he's sharing his mistakes so that you can avoid making the same ones yourself. I'm not going to do that in *Zero Negativity*. I want to show you that if you never make mistakes in life, you never make anything. Nobody in the history of the world has ever been perfect. Nobody. You'll never be perfect, and that's OK, that's human. But what you *can* become is the best version of yourself. Fucking up can be as valuable to your personal development as any university course. I needed to find myself in a position where I was making the same stupid mistakes over and over again – getting into fights, drinking heavily – before I reached rock bottom. And if I hadn't sunk to those depths, I know for sure that I wouldn't be in the position I'm in now.

There's nothing complex about my philosophy. If you tackle a negative situation with a positive mindset, you'll find a solution. If you tackle a positive situation with a positive mindset, then it's win–win: you'll be through the clouds. So why wouldn't you give yourself that built-in advantage? Why would you want to tackle anything in life with negativity? Having a negative mindset effectively means tying one hand behind your back.

Sometimes I ask people, 'Have you ever been excited about waking up?' Very often, I'll know the answer before it's even left their lips.

'No.'

'What, *never* in your life? Not even on Christmas Day when you were a kid?'

'Well, yeah, of course.'

'You were in a positive mindset then, because you were going to get presents and eat turkey. They're feelings you'll never forget.'

'For sure.'

'Then why don't you have them now? You don't put yourself in the right situations, you don't grab opportunities, you don't think positively.'

Most kids are naturally positive, whereas a lot of adults seem to have dedicated large portions of their life to deleting their capacity for positivity. We're told to worry about exams, we're told that we're not bringing up our children right, we're told that we should have a particular kind of job by a particular point in our life, we're told that we should be climbing up the property ladder. Conformity to these sorts of ideas is imposed upon us, and its effect is often very negative. You're expected to get in line with all these things, and you get so involved in doing so that you develop a one-track vision. We get so focused on the path that others have laid out in front of us that we forget to ever look up and take in the world around us.

We need to rediscover that excitement we felt when we were a kid, when the world appeared big and exciting, and everything seemed new and full of adventure. As most people get older, their horizons narrow; they tend to think more about what they can't do than what they can.

I'm different. I'll try to seize a positive from any negative situation that comes along. Sometimes it's obvious, sometimes it's not. Sometimes you don't think you've been able to extract any benefit until, having parked it up, three or four years down the line you realise its significance or how it connects to other elements in your life. If you're a positive person, you can leave negative experiences on the shelf, safe in the knowledge that they'll come in handy one day. They're there, but you don't let them distract you.

Over time I've trained my mind so that I approach every situation I'm in with a positive mindset. It comes naturally, without thinking. I've got to the point where I'm such a positive thinker that I'm permanently convinced that good things will come my way. If I told you what I see when I look ahead towards my future, you'd think I was an absolute madman. All I see are bright lights. And that was as true when I was in my prison cell, or sitting in the pissing wet of an Afghan hillside, as it is now.

When I left prison in 2013 I had £10.52 to my name. Nothing, really. But I was excited. I was at the bottom, and I knew I only had one way to go. I've got a rock-solid foundation now and I'm building, building, building. Charities, tech companies, clothing brands. I want everything life can give me.

I can see how some people might think I'm delusional. But I'm a realist. I believe I can get there. I can back everything up. I know I'm willing to work, sacrifice and suffer to get to the place I want to reach. I'm willing to try and fail, try and fail, try and fail until I get it right. I've got so much positive energy now that I sometimes feel as if you could run the National Grid off me.

What I want to do in this book is help you tap into the same.

Everything I do now – books, TV programmes, speaking tours – it's all because I want to help people develop and make them realise what they're capable of. I'm fascinated by people, I'm fascinated by their potential, and also by the fact that most of us only use a quarter of our power. I find that really frustrating. Negativity is the thing that, maybe more than any other factor, will put a limit on your ability to be the best version of yourself you can be.

The good news is that you're not doomed to negativity. There's a way out. Everybody can train themselves to think positively and tackle negative situations with a positive mindset. It just takes a concerted effort. You may not feel positive all the time – nobody does – and yet eventually you reach a point where you're automatically tackling every situation with a positive mindset. It takes time and it requires brutal honesty, but it's worth it. While I'd never say that you'll be invincible, I guarantee that not much will faze you.

Once you've mastered a positive mindset, you'll be *excited* to take on negative situations because you'll be desperate to see what their outcome will be. You'll see them as opportunities to discover where the limits of your potential lie and as chances to learn new skills, experience new things.

When a positive situation comes along, and you dive into it with a positive mindset, you'll feel like you're flying, or as if you've been transported to another dimension. I often experience extended phases of complete euphoria, riding the clouds with Zeus looking down on the world, endorphins racing through my veins. It can get to the point where I can't even get to sleep because I'm so excited about getting up the following morning and re-attacking life. This mood can last for weeks, each day speeding past in the blink of an eye.

Living a life with zero negativity has many physical benefits. It will encourage you to follow a healthier, more productive lifestyle. Studies show that positive people get more physical activity, eat a better diet and are less likely to smoke or drink alcohol to excess. In addition to this, current research shows that positive thinking can confer many health benefits, including lower rates of depression and psychological distress, greater resistance to the common cold and reduced risk of death from cardiovascular disease. They even think it will help you live longer. And the more positive you are, the better your relationships with everyone around you will be.

Being negative is isolating. Negative individuals don't tend to have many friends. By contrast, positivity attracts other people. When you're positive, you'll find that others just want to be around you – it's as if you've become magnetic. And being around somebody who exudes positivity is the most powerful thing. It can feel tiring at times because they'll be a mass of whirring energy, but you'll come away with excitement and inspiration pumping through your veins.

These are all good things, but it's the mental advantages positivity can offer that I'm most interested in, and which will be the focus of this book. In the chapters that follow I'll show you how to embrace failure and use it to your advantage, how to learn to see change as the foundation of your future success, how to develop resilience, how to deal with bullies online and offline, what it means to be a positive father, how to make and seize opportunities for yourself, and how to live a life with no regrets. I'm not here to tell you who to be, where you should live or what job you should do. All that is up to you. What I do want to do, however, is to give you the tools you need to become the best possible version of yourself.

One last thing. My voice isn't the only one you'll hear in these pages. Each chapter will feature my wife Emilie's take on whichever subject I've been talking about. My life has been improved a million times over by her kind, measured, no-bullshit perspective. I'm sure that yours will be too.

CHAPTER 1

I KNOW WHO I AM

AHEAD OF SERIES 4 of *SAS: Who Dares Wins*, one of the producers asked me in for a meeting. 'Ant,' she said, 'how do you feel about us changing things up a bit?'

Not long before we met, the British Army had announced that, from that point on, women would be allowed to apply for every single role in the military, including combat roles, with the Royal Marines doing likewise. For the first time in its history, recruitment would be decided by ability alone, and gender wouldn't have anything to do with it. The producer had suggested that we should follow suit and include female contestants.

Initially, every instinct told me to steer clear. 'I'm not sure,' I told her. 'This isn't for us to do. It's going to be complex – maybe it would be better if we left this to the army and Marines?'

I could see my producer was still thinking about it. Then she surprised me by asking me what it was I looked for in recruits for the show.

This was an easy one to answer: 'I'm looking for all-round, balanced individuals.' As soon as I said it, I realised something: that last word. It doesn't matter if it's a male or female – it's about an *individual*. What's most important is that they're somebody who knows themselves better than anybody else; somebody who knows their strengths, but who also acknowledges that they have weaknesses and insecurities. Within hours of the start of filming I saw how tough, driven and resilient the female contestants were. It was eye-opening to watch the way they threw themselves heart and soul into every challenge. They fought as hard as the men, maybe harder. I instantly regretted my original reluctance. Having women alongside men added a completely different dimension to the programme.

The whole show is about putting all the contestants under a microscope, exposing them to such high levels of stress that they're forced to confront elements of their personality that they've tried to keep hidden. Many discover talents within themselves that they never knew existed, others are surprised to find fault lines that, under pressure, start to crack apart. There's no contestant, no matter how far into the competition they get, who comes away without a greater understanding of every aspect of their personality. What I realised was that I still had lots to learn too.

If there was any positive to be gained from the upheaval and distress of my early years, it was that during that period I picked up the habit of self-reflection. Like the men and women trying to get through to the end of *SAS: Who Dares Wins*, an intense period of disorientation and discomfort helped me gain a new knowledge of myself. If I'd had a more normal upbringing, I bet I'd have continued on a happy, oblivious path, like most kids.

Instead, there was my father's death, and its unsettling, disorienting aftermath, when within days my mum married a new man, Dean, and every detail about Dad was wiped from our lives. Even his picture was taken off the walls. There were some days when it could seem as if he'd never existed at all. Or, at least, that's what the adults in our house appeared to want us to pretend. His money was still good, though. The family lived it up for a bit in Portsmouth, using his life insurance payout, which took us from a council house to a big fancy home and private schools. Then everything turned upside again in the blink of an eye.

It was never actually clear to me and my siblings what prompted the sudden move to another country. There was a feud of some kind between my mum's and late dad's sides of my family. We were mostly protected from it, but we could all tell that something was going on off stage. So perhaps that had something to do with it.

One cold, damp winter's day when I was nine, my mum picked me up from school early in the afternoon. I was a bit surprised as she didn't normally come at this time, so I asked her what was going on. She said, 'Dean's patio firm has burned down.' She was strangely calm and matter of fact. Even at that age I was knocked a bit off balance by this.

'What do you mean?'

'It's all gone, burned to the ground.'

We drove over to the factory. Cinders and ash were every-where. The fire brigade had already been and so some things were only half-burned, just about standing. In the middle of it all was my stepdad Dean. He was clearly distressed, pick-ing up horribly stained patio slabs and then throwing them down in disgust. He kept on saying, 'All that work. All that work.'

Apparently there had been an electrical fault. With the business literally up in flames, Dean and my mum decided that when the insurance money came through, they would move the whole family off to rural France.

Portsmouth is a working city. It's busy and vibrant, full of builders, bricklayers and scaffolders. And it's as British as they come. Going from there to a small village in Normandy was a lot for us to take in. All of a sudden we'd swapped the densely packed bungalows and villas of England's south coast for rambling open countryside. I'd been used to crowded cul-de-sacs, bustling high streets, the chatter of passers-by. Now we were surrounded by endless land, space and quiet.

Our new home was an ancient farm with a huge barn next to it. Dean threw himself into remaking the whole house, which was in a fucking state, almost a wreck. In those first few months while he tried to make it liveable, we slept and ate in caravans that were parked up in the barn.

That was when it all hit me. I remember asking myself: where did the good life go? How come we're living in a *barn*? You can deal with change when it's a question of moving two streets, even two towns, away. But starting your whole life again? That's something else, especially when, like me, you're still grieving for a dead father. There were other strange things that I couldn't get my head around. We were eating pasta and sweetcorn for breakfast, lunch and dinner. I was being dressed in hand-me-down shoes and clothes from my brothers. And the adults were driving a shitty old car that occasionally would simply refuse to start. But on the other hand, the house Dean was working on was massive.

To begin with, this strangeness was compounded by the exhilarating freedom my brothers and I discovered in our newfound isolation. We'd moved in summer, and since Dean and our mum were so focused on getting things up and running, we were given the run of the fields around the house. Nobody told us what we could or couldn't do. Even sleeping in a caravan was like an adventure after suburban Portsmouth.

And then it all came to an end. The threat of going to a French Catholic school had hung over us right through July and August, but we'd managed to shove it to the backs of our minds. I didn't speak a word of French, not even stuff like *bonjour* or *au revoir*. We were also going to be the first English children to ever attend the school. New kids are always treated like they're carrying a disease – surely the fact that we were foreign would make that even worse.

On the first day of school we were late – the fucking car wouldn't start. I can vividly remember going into the classroom. I walked in and there was a moment of silence. Every single pair of eyes in the classroom bored right into me. The way those rows of kids were staring at me – it was as if I'd murdered somebody. My cheeks went red, but it was going to get worse. On the way in, once it had become clear that we were going to be late, I'd asked my two older brothers how to explain that we'd had the problem with the car. They told me, 'Just say, "*voiture kaput*".' This would have been good advice, but what they hadn't told me was that you have to pronounce '*kaput*' as 'kapoot'. If you say 'kapot', people will think you're saying '*capote*', which is a French word for condom.

I went into the classroom in the middle of a French lesson being taught by Monsieur Laurent, the headmaster, who was bald, with glasses and a polo neck – he looked as French as you like – and who ran the school along with his wife (because it was a Catholic school, the majority of the staff were nuns, something that added an extra layer of weirdness as I walked in). Madame Laurent was known as the good cop, while her husband was the bad cop. The tradition there was that if you were late, you had to stand up in front of the class and explain why. Schools are stricter in France, especially religious ones. I was dragged up in front of the blackboard, and then Monsieur Laurent spoke some words in French to me. I looked blankly back at him. I had no idea what he was saying. He repeated his question, in English this time: 'Why were you late?'

That's when I said the only French words I knew: '*Voiture kaput.*' Except, of course, not knowing any better, I said 'kapot'. The whole class burst into laughter, and I just stood there, bewildered, with no idea what was going on. Then Monsieur Laurent put me out of my misery and escorted me to my chair. I sat there humiliated and angry, and increasingly anxious about what was to come next.

It was the longest day of my life. Everything was strange. Everything was a challenge. Going into the playground that very first break time I found that I was an object of fascination. Most of the other kids crowding around me had never met anyone from England. This was La Manche, Normandy, a place where a lost cow or a surprisingly big chicken could end up as the talk of the town. It was two hundred miles in distance, and about a century in time, from Paris.

To them I was a freakshow. One minute they were all laughing at me, the next they were firing a million incomprehensible questions in my direction. One thing they kept asking me was if I wanted to play '*babyfoot*'. I now know that this means table football, but at the time I thought they were warning me that we'd be having baby food for lunch. So when it was time for the rest of the kids to go to the cafeteria, I just found somewhere to hide. Going hungry seemed to me a better option than cramming mush down my throat.

I remember crouching down, asking myself again and again, 'What the *fuck* is going on?'

WHEN WE GOT back to our home later that afternoon I went straight to the den we'd made in the massive conifer trees at the bottom of the garden. I crawled in there in my school uniform and curled up, watching cars whooshing past on the main road from Caen to Saint-Lô, counting them, thinking, 'How am I going to get through this? What is the solution?'

Ultimately, though, there wasn't a solution. Or, maybe there was one, but finding it was way above my pay grade. My mum and stepdad might have been able to choose to go back, or change things up again, but I didn't have that power. I was just a kid

What I realised was: you just have to go along with things. You're at that school, whether you like it or not. You're living in France, whether you like it or not. You've got to fucking adapt to it – or you crumble. If I didn't get on with it, I'd have never gone back to school again. And it wasn't like I could escape it for long; there were even classes on

Saturday mornings. But if I couldn't change the situation, I could change the way I *perceived* it.

In the process I developed a habit that has stayed with me to this day. The magnitude of the situation was so overwhelming that I could not possibly begin to understand it, although I did comprehend that there was a new man in my family's life and that we were in a new country where they spoke a different language.

I remember thinking: don't try to understand what you can't. The only thing I could understand was myself. I began self-reflecting. I couldn't control anything about being in France, I couldn't change the sheer fact of our location, but I could look inside myself and see what tools I had to face the situation.

I say this to my children even now. 'What makes sense to you? What can you understand?' They'll tell me what they can understand, and I'll say to them: 'Everything else, don't even try. At this time in your life it's too much to take in. Wait until you're older.'

That's what I did. When I couldn't understand why my father had died so young and had been replaced so quickly by another man, I cut it out and focused more on myself. I could control what I was doing and feeling. You cannot expect to have the answers all the time, so why torment and confuse yourself by pretending otherwise? It will all make sense in time, when you're ready. Don't waste years of your life.

Sitting there, in my den, I asked myself: do you want to be that boy hiding from lunch every single day? Why not just embrace being that country kid? The moment you start fighting against it rather than looking for opportunities, that's the moment you start to go under. I began to list my strengths and weaknesses to myself. I knew I was good at getting on with people, I was good at football (a handy thing for helping you fit in with other kids at the best of times, and even more so when you had no common language), I was resilient. These were all strengths I knew I could draw on and develop. But I couldn't speak French and I didn't have much leverage over my circumstances. These were both weaknesses. As I thought about it, I understood that while one of these could be fixed the other couldn't. Just acknowledging that fact lifted a weight from my shoulders.

The next day I went into school almost without a care in the world. I stopped worrying and my attitude became far more, 'Let's just see how this goes.' I went into lunch and realised that the food was actually decent, and went into what was called the foyer and found out what *babyfoot* really was. I played football in the yard with the other children and began to form a connection with them. My first and second days were like chalk and cheese.

I worked on the things that lay within my power, like getting to school on time, and I didn't stress about the things that weren't. I knew I wasn't going to learn French overnight, so I didn't allow myself to get dispirited by getting bad results to begin with. It wasn't that I didn't care; it was more that I was aware of what I could and couldn't control, and so realised that there was no value whatsoever in beating myself up about stuff that wasn't in my hands.

This habit of self-reflection was just what I needed. I'd go to school during the day, mix with the French kids, sit through all the lessons, then I'd come home and play in the den. It was almost as if I had two lives. On the one hand I was like a young Robinson Crusoe, running wild in the countryside, on the other I was receiving this really old-school French education.

And it worked. Back in England, school had never interested me and I never took lessons seriously. I didn't play up in class; it was more that I was a daydreamer with the attention span of a gnat. But because I'd been plonked down in a French school, I picked the language up pretty quickly. I was surrounded by it, so I didn't really have to try. Within three months I was holding perfect conversations without any trouble at all. Within six I might as well have been French. I had a Normandy accent. Some people refused to believe I was English. Years later, when I was in the military and doing work with the French Foreign Legion, the guys there thought I was some sort of undercover agent.

It was there, in France, as a lost and confused kid, that I began the process of really understanding myself and the world around me. I felt alone, and knew that I couldn't rely on anybody else. I learned that everything starts with yourself. To begin with, that responsibility was daunting. Now, I realise how exciting and liberating it really is.

'ANT, WHO ARE YOU?'

One thing I do sometimes when I give talks is get somebody up on stage and ask them, 'Who are you?' The answer is always something along the lines of, 'I'm John. I'm a software engineer. I've got four kids and a wife.'

So I ask the same question again: 'Who are you?' They'll be a bit less sure this time round. 'I'm John, I'm a software engineer, and I'm a loving husband.' At this point I flip it around.

'Ask me who *I* am.'

'Ant, who are you?'

'I'm an emotionally connected, positive, driven individual. That's who I am. What you told me are only the labels other people have given you. You're John. Somebody has given you that name. Software engineer? That's a job title, it's not who you are. However, you saying you're a loving husband; that's closer to the truth. Are you an emotional person? Are you empathetic? Do you think positively? Who are you?'

Sometimes they'll still struggle to articulate who they are outside of the names other people have given them. Others will be different. They'll say, 'Well, to be honest, I'm pretty negative. I worry I can be selfish.'

That's when I know I've got them. Fucking hell. You've come to the right place. Most people don't really know themselves. Worse than that, they're not even interested in getting to know themselves. They're perfectly happy just bobbing along on autopilot.

If you do that, you're depriving yourself of the possibility of becoming the best possible version of yourself. It means you'll never be able to be properly honest with yourself, and you'll lose out on so many opportunities and possibilities. Life is just going to pass you by.

There's so much about the world that you can't control, it can feel overwhelming. That's certainly how I felt on that shitty first day at the French school. What *is* in your hands, however, is your ability to look inside yourself. When you take the time to get to know yourself better than anybody else on the planet, you'll be building the foundations of positivity. It's not always easy, and it can sometimes involve ripping yourself to pieces in the most brutal way possible, but, fuck me, when you've done that you'll know it will have been worthwhile. When you've identified your weakness and strengths, you can then begin to focus on the positive parts of your personality. And when you do this, everything else, all the negatives, will just get dragged along behind you.

CELEBRATE YOUR STRENGTHS

If you've taken the time to identify what your strengths are, then make the most of them. Don't give in to doubt or fear. There's no trait more positive than believing in your own abilities. If you're good at something, then celebrate it. The confidence you gain from knowing that you have a particular skill, or excel at a particular sport, or are just adept at getting on with people, is a tangible force; it infuses everything you do, makes you more decisive, your movements more sure. The more confident you are in what you can do, the more likely you are to succeed.

When I was in the Special Forces I respected the enemy, but I also knew that I was a hundred times more dangerous than them. There weren't many in the British armed forces who were better at their trade than me; what chance did an untrained insurgent – most likely a country boy – have? Most of the time it was like a duck shoot. Even the hardcore militants we sometimes came across, who had a bit more about them – the guys who knew how to move, who could aim their weapons – there was nothing they could do that I couldn't do better. That's not arrogance. It was a fact, backed up night after night, in operation after operation. That's why, when I went out there, I genuinely never thought I'd get hit. Knowing my strengths, and being confident in them, made me a better soldier.

By contrast, if you're plagued by doubts and don't have faith in yourself, the chances are that things will go wrong. There was a guy in my unit who got shot every time he went into combat: his leg, his arm. He got blown out of his wagon one tour, and on another he got hit in the arse while trying to crawl behind cover. On one level, it was just rank bad luck. On another, I knew that he was a real worrier, enough to make me wonder whether he was attracting that negativity. It happened too often to be a coincidence, and finally reached the point where he simply didn't want to go on tour anymore.

All of this is just as relevant in day-to-day life. If you've been offered a great new job, celebrate that fact. Use it as an opportunity to remind yourself that there's a reason why that company chose you over all the other applicants. The moment you start telling yourself that you don't deserve the job, or that they made a mistake giving it to you, is the moment that you allow negativity to become the dominant force in your head. When you convince yourself that you can't do the job, you're likely to make that fear a self-fulfilling prophecy. Almost before you know it, you'll have turned a great positive into a crushing negative.

THE HAMMER OF THOR

I always get people asking me what's the most frightening situation I've been in. I think they expect I'll tell them about a time when I've been under fire, or in hand-to-hand combat. But it's not.

Courage isn't about walking through a door with bullets flying. That was just a question of top-level training and being good at a job that I loved. No, courage is the ability to be honest with yourself. The most frightening, exhilarating place anyone can be is a space in which they're being entirely, brutally honest with themselves. It's the hardest thing you can do. It's also the best thing you can do.

If you're honest with yourself, you can be honest with other people and about the situations you find yourself in. If you're honest about the situation, you'll be able to identify whether it's a positive or negative. When you're able to identify something as a negative situation, you should also be able to step back long enough to realise that the only way to deal with it is with a positive mindset.

Don't get me wrong. Being open with yourself is tough – it involves ripping yourself to bits, pulling and pulling and pulling until you've found all of your weaknesses and insecurities. You might want to pretend that your weaknesses don't exist, but that's *you*. Do you want to be 60 per cent of yourself for the rest of your life? There might be 10 per cent of your personality that will remain forever negative. The rest, though? Isn't it worth trying? If you don't challenge your weaknesses, how will you ever find out whether it's possible to turn them into strengths? You don't want to be one of those people who just do what they're good at until the day they die. That's the equivalent of only eating McDonald's; it's easy, relatively cheap and immediately satisfying. Ultimately, however, it's not as nutritious and satisfying as a meal you've spent hours preparing. Honesty is maybe the most powerful tool you have in your toolbox. It's also unquestionably the hardest one to use. It's such a direct way of confronting negativity.

So many people say to me, 'My problems would be solved if only I could be honest with my wife' … or my husband or my boss or my mother. They see the risk of offending people as outweighing the positivity that would come with actually fixing a negative situation.

Honesty is the skeleton key that can open so many doors, but people – and I can understand why – are unwilling to use it. They'd prefer to find other means to pick locks. My view is that you should see it like ripping a plaster off. It will be painful for a short while, but just *do* it.

Precisely because it's so powerful, honesty can be detrimental in the wrong hands. There are some people who will try to use the truth to annihilate you. They have no intention of bringing you back up; all they want it to bring you down. It's a bit like Thor – that hammer won't come to him unless he's using it for pure reasons. When he does get to wield it, though: wow, think of everything he can do!

EMBRACE CRITICISM

One of the challenges that wrongfoots a lot of the recruits on *Who Dares Wins* is when we invite them to identify the weakest members of the group. It's a brutal exercise, one that's as much of a shock to them as some of the gruelling physical tasks. We do it halfway through the course, so that they're no longer strangers and have had the chance to assess each other's weaknesses and strengths. Calling others out like that is something that most people aren't used to. It's almost a taboo. I watch incredibly carefully to see how they respond.

The negative contestants will find an excuse to block that criticism out. They'll get back into the room and pretend to be untroubled by it. They'll say, like Louise in Series 5, 'Oh, I knew that it was going to be happen, it's all part of the game. It doesn't bother me. I know who I am.'

In my eyes, that's a mistake. If you've got five or six rivals telling you that you're weak, you should take it as a positive. If they're saying they think you'll be the one to let them down, why is that? If it were me, I'd want to know *exactly* why they'd picked me out. Is it because I get overwhelmed by nerves? Is it because I'm not mixing properly?

What they should do is, first off, not let that criticism overwhelm them. They're in a really unfamiliar situation, one that they're desperately trying to figure out as they go along, so of course they're going to get things wrong – the whole point of the show is to put them under so much pressure that their fault lines emerge. Once they've done that, it's time to be honest and take that criticism on board – no matter how harsh or hurtful it might be – and change themselves accordingly.

Now that I'm in the public eye, I'm exposed to a lot more criticism than I've previously been used to. For instance, I have to make decisions about whether, and how, I'll respond to press stories about me, especially those that twist my words out of context. The first emotion I always experience on reading the nonsense that gets written is anger. This is followed very quickly by a strong desire to turn up at their offices and call them out for a bunch of lying twats. It's entirely natural to want to do that. It would also be entirely counter-productive. It wouldn't achieve anything apart from causing more trouble.

That's why I've learned to listen to another voice. This one reminds me that while I know what I've done and what I've been through, and that I know who I am as a person, the people criticising me or twisting my words don't. So why should I care what they think or say?

It's the same for me with social media. If it's some keyboard warrior who's never met me, I don't care what they say. It's their negative thoughts, not mine. I'm not going to allow my mood to be dictated by the opinions of someone who knows they're a safe distance away from me and therefore feels entitled to run their mouth off. If they're somebody I used to know a long time ago but is no longer part of my circle, again I won't let it trouble me. They're probably right, I probably was a fucking nightmare back in the day. But why's that relevant now? Is it who I am now? No. I ignore it. I don't need another reminder of how many people are riddled with negativity. I went to prison because I tried to help out somebody I'd never met before, and where did that get me? Nowhere. So why would I ever rise to something that could potentially rile me up or put me into a negative headspace?

And yet when it's somebody whom I do care about, who's in my circle, then of course I listen. The people who love you will offer you *constructive* criticism, because they want you to be the best version of yourself that you can be. They know you're better than that. They know what you're worth. They're not having a pop because they want to bring you down a peg or two. It's also worth remembering that not only will they have a different set of life experiences to you – and so have a different way of approaching things. They'll also have that little bit of distance that means they can give you a different perspective on your behaviour, or the way that you come across.

You owe it to yourself to be honest when those closest to you and those you most trust pick you up on something. My attitude on those occasions is, 'Right, I need to fix this, need to concentrate on it, make sure I don't do it again.' You should see that sort of criticism as a positive thing, because it should lead to improvement.

LISTEN TO THE VOICE IN YOUR HEAD

The voice you hear in your head is the true 'you' ripping yourself to shreds. It never lies to you. If you're already brutally honest with yourself, then nothing that this voice says will come as a surprise. Instead, you should treat it as motivation. It gains its own power when you use it as a spur to action. If I do something stupid at work and everybody else tells me not to worry, nothing *that* bad has happened. But the voice in my head is harsher – 'Ant, I'm not sure about the way you behaved today. You could have approached this whole situation completely differently' – then that's the message I'm going to take away. Of course, it's no good if you don't follow through, because that's when it will leave you feeling negative, or low.

There was a night at an awards ceremony recently when, without having made any conscious decision to do so, I found that I'd slipped into the role of 'chief instructor'. I'd been a bit nervous beforehand, so I'd had a couple of drinks. Then, when the people around me started discussing the show, I responded by being loud and talking too much;

boasting, talking about violence. I was trying to be the person that I thought that they wanted me to be. Even then, though, I could see a couple of people saying to themselves, 'Oh, for fuck's sake.' The next morning, when I looked back on it, I knew I hadn't been myself. I knew I must have sounded like a right knobhead.

When I hear my conscience speaking to me, that's my cue to say, 'Fuck, right, I better do something about this. Why did I behave like that? Because you had too much to drink last night, Ant, and you hadn't drunk for six months before that, so you acted like a twat. Next time, you'll do things differently. You'll be cool, calm and collected, the person you really are.' Once I've been through that process, then that's it, I don't dwell on it. First, because the damage has been done, and there's nothing I can do about it now. And second, because I'm using the cringeworthy memory of me behaving badly as motivation to make sure I'm never like that again.

The voices in your head are only saying what you already know. You don't have another being living inside you; it's you, and you're the only person who can change the script that voice is reading from. It can be fucking horrible, but listen to it; it usually has a point.

WORK ON YOUR WEAKNESSES

If you've got a weakness that's stopping you from getting to where you want to go, it's up to you to work on it. Don't just use its existence as an excuse.

There are lots of hard things about being a sniper, such as staying switched on and not falling asleep during the endless waiting, and the difficulty of calculating wind speed when you finally get your target in your sights. But the hardest thing for me was staying still. I'm a fidget and I've got an overactive mind. What's next? What's next? What's next? I can't sit still.

I've always been like that. Every basic training I've ever been through I've got into trouble at some point during the drill stages. I couldn't stand still. I'd have to move, I'd have to look, I'd have to do something. Too. Much. Energy.

I remember when I was still a seventeen-year-old, nine-stone whippersnapper about to pass out through basic training. We were on the parade square going through the rehearsal for the following day's ceremony and I'd just gone up to the front to pretend to accept the awards for best recruit and best PT. There was so much emphasis on the way we looked, the way we stood, even the expressions on our faces. For the NCOs who'd been tasked with bringing us up to scratch, anything other than a perfect performance was an outrage. And a perfect performance involved staying

49

stock-still in those moments when we were supposed to be standing at attention.

It was during one of these moments when I was standing there, happy, thinking, 'Tomorrow we pass out, this is fucking great. People are going to be really proud of me.' That was when the drill corporal loomed over my shoulder. 'Middleton, if you fucking move again, I'm going to march you to the fucking guardroom and you'll spend the night in a fucking cell. And then you'll go straight to the parade from the cell, looking like a fucking reprobate who has spent the night in a cell.'

I must have been moving some part of my body without realising it. Fuck. 'Yes, corporal!' What else could I say? I tried. I really tried, but I couldn't help myself. I moved again. Just a tiny little flash of my eyes from one side to the other, but that was enough for the drill sergeant.

'Fuuuuuucking Middleton, stand to attention! Left wheel! Follow me! You're sleeping in the cell tonight.'

I stood to attention. Then marched off. That was when the troop sergeant spotted us, and called me and the corporal over. It was as if he couldn't resist getting in on the 'Shouting at Middleton' game.

'What the fuck are you doing? Why can't you stand fucking still? If you weren't such a good fucking soldier I fucking promise you that you'd spend the fucking night in that fucking cell. Don't let yourself down, you're a fucking *fidget*.' At that point he stopped bellowing, and in a quieter, almost confiding voice, he carried on. 'Fidgets are good in the military, just not on my parade square. File back in. You've got five minutes left. Do not. Fucking. Move.'

It was uncanny. Almost exactly the same thing happened during Royal Marine training. Once again I'd been awarded best recruit – they called it the King's Badge – and we were having an inspection of our Lovats, one of the two uniforms we'd be wearing during the next day's ceremony.

I was standing there, proud about the wings I'd earned during my time in the Paras and the diamond I'd been given during the course I was just about to complete, and as the CO stalked around the lines of Marines he kept looking at me. Couldn't take his eyes off me, it seemed. I thought it was because he knew that I was going to be awarded the King's Badge. Of course, it was because while every other Marine there was motionless, I was practically running on the spot. As my wife said to me later, 'Ant, you might as well have been breakdancing.'

Then the CO came up to me. 'Middleton, you're the King's Badge, aren't you?'

'Yes, sir.'

'Are you excited?'

'Not really, sir. I'm more proud, to be honest.'

'So why are you moving so much? Every time I turn around you're wriggling about. You cannot stand still.'

There are worse weaknesses to have. But it's still a weakness, especially for somebody who wanted to train as a sniper. Sniping is hardcore soldiering, a lethal, physically and mentally demanding game of chess. A sniper who knows his trade can use the fear he inspires to stop an overwhelming force in its tracks. Yes please, I thought. This sounds cool. This sounds *exciting*.

When the course began it was clear that I was good at the bits that others found tricky. I loved the stalking and crawling around, because it meant I could move and be active. The fly in the ointment was that I was shit at the thing that the rest of the guys found pretty simple. Staying. Fucking. Still. I had to admit to myself that if I indulged in the temptation to keep moving at all times, I'd put my chances of being allowed to do a job I desperately wanted at risk. I'd put so much into getting to this point, I didn't want to throw all that away.

So, in response, I was relentless in developing the discipline and willpower I needed to be able to lie still in an observation post. I told myself: *Now is when the hard work starts. Make this count.* I practised it over and over and over, until even the idea of being motionless made me feel sick. I'd get into my lay-up position, stay still for a couple of minutes, then my knee would jiggle or my arm would twitch. Caught again. Back into my lay-up position. Ten minutes this time, then the smallest movement of my head. Fuck, caught *again*. But I improved every time I tried. Eventually, after failing more times than I could count, I got there. What helped me do this was my mindset. I had a positive motivator, and this meant I could keep on pushing, even when, at the beginning, it seemed as if I might never get there.

But I knew there were limits to what discipline and will-power could achieve. When I got back from Afghanistan they wanted to send me on a course designed to transform me into a surveillance operator. I told them, 'Sorry, no, I can't do that.'

I knew myself well enough to be aware that I could summon up the brief stretches of discipline necessary to control myself every now and then on a sniper mission. I'd worked on it relentlessly and I could suck it up. But although it was a skill I'd trained myself to develop, it never came easy. Am I a door-kicker? Yes. Could I sit in a car and go unnoticed for days on end? Absolutely no fucking chance.

STEERING CLEAR

You don't need to fix every flaw. I suffer from claustrophobia – not an ideal condition to have when you're in the Special Forces.

It's not a crippling problem. I'm OK in crowds, but could you put me into the boot of a car without me flipping out? No. Could I spend any meaningful time in a small caving tunnel? No.

A small lift is enough to bring me close to a panic attack – those moments when you find yourself taking long, deliberate breaths to try to keep yourself calm. I hate the lack of control. When I get into those situations, I'm immediately looking for the exit route. If I enter a lift and I know I'm completely locked in, that's when I say to myself, 'Fuck, if something goes wrong, I'm going to have to prise those doors open. Breathe, breathe, breathe, breathe: whatever you do, don't stop.' If there's a little cubby hole, something that gives me more space to escape, then I'm OK with it.

If I'm crawling through a tunnel and I can see a light at its end, I'm fine. I know there'll be enough air. If it's bendy and I can't see the exit, then I'm in trouble and I know I'll have to work really hard to calm myself down.

I've got better and better at coping with claustrophobia over the years. In my old life there were times when I'd no choice but to put myself through it, and on those occasions I was able to exert the self-control needed to succeed. Now, however, I've reached a point where I ask myself: how much of my life am I really going to be spending in these sorts of small, confined spaces? The answer is: not much. So is it worth expending vast amounts of my time and energy confronting this fear? Probably not. It doesn't affect my career, it's not stopping me from being a good husband or father and it's not preventing me doing anything I love.

When I struggled with fear and found myself not wanting to go back to Afghanistan, I had to confront it, because I risked losing everything I loved doing. I had to ask myself if

I was willing to sacrifice my training, the belonging I felt as part of that unit, to the fact that I was scared. No, I wasn't willing to abandon any of it, so I worked on it, I challenged it until I had defeated it. Claustrophobia is different. At the time, it was manageable and I knew I could just drag it along with me. Now I simply steer clear of any situation where I think I'm likely to feel that discomfort.

My mate's a fireman and three times he's said to me, 'Ant, I've OK'd it with the boss. You can go down the rat run and we'll pump smoke through the little pipes as you crawl through them.' Every time I've been really enthusiastic for a little while, and every time I've put it off. There are better things I can do with my time. Much better things. In fact, I couldn't think of anything *worse* than being trapped in a smoked-out room, wearing the whole firefighter's apparatus, and trying to squeeze through a series of tiny holes. With people in front and behind me? Fuck. That.

With other people, I can see that it might be different – I know that there are huge variations in the fears and emotions experienced by everybody. If you're afraid of flying, you'll probably be able to live much of your life quite happily without that fear impinging on you. But what if you want to go on holiday abroad? It's going to be something you're going to have to deal with. Especially if the alternative is a week away in Grimsby.

FIND YOUR POSITIVE MOTIVATOR

Your positive motivator is the thing that will drag you through even the toughest of times, giving you the inspiration you need to make the most of your strengths and overcome your weaknesses.

People have come to me so many times and complained about how much effort they've wasted on a particular situation and got nowhere. The answer is usually obvious – the missing ingredient is almost always positivity. They'll say, 'How the fuck am I supposed to think positively when I can't dig myself out of this hole?' My answer will invariably be, 'You're stuck there *because* you're not thinking positively.'

They've got all these other elements, which are great; but they're running on negative fuel, and they've got nothing to give them a positive motivator, a light at the end of the tunnel. It's only positivity – the positivity that only *you* can provide – that will tie all your effort and drive together, and keep you bouncing back.

My positive motivator is my family. I want to be the best version of myself so that I can be a good role model for them and provide a secure, happy foundation for them to go on and thrive. I have to work hard for this – eighty-hour weeks, months at a time away from Emilie and the kids – but having this positive motivator means that I'm willing to endure whatever sacrifices I need to make. I know I'll constantly need to evolve and change to get there; but that's fine, because I know it will be worth it.

Take time to work out what you really want from life. It's by looking inside yourself, interrogating your priorities, really examining your ambitions, that you'll find your positive motivator. Above all, you have to be honest with yourself. Success for some people is a big house and a nice car. However, you should be wary of reducing your positive motivator to a shopping list. The material things that have come my way are great, and I appreciate them; it's just that I see them as the by-products of success rather than an end in themselves. Do you really want the sole aim of your existence to be acquiring a new Mercedes? Will that provide you with the fulfilment you need? Only you can answer that question.

POSITIVE THINKING IS SMART THINKING

Positive thinking is also, to a large extent, smart thinking. It's not about indiscriminate, undirected energy. People think that resilience is all about grit and determination. They're big parts of it, but as I see it, a willingness to run through walls is, at best, only a start. If you don't inject positivity into that it will soon wear thin. It will run out or, worse, curdle into negativity. You'll tell yourself that you've tried and failed, so what's the point?

There was a good example of this on the latest celebrity edition of *SAS: Who Dares Wins*. I'll always give people a chance, no matter how negative they might appear at first glance. It's stupid to write people off immediately, and everybody deserves another go. It's a principle that I try to put into practice in the show. If we gave up on contestants when they first made a mistake or disappointed us in some way, then by episode six it would just be us instructors griping at each other, and nobody wants to watch that. I want to give them space to work things out for themselves, be honest with themselves. Am I doing this for the right reasons? If the answer is no, do you want to prolong the suffering, because you know the outcome? I can help them towards their decision, but I can't make it for them. Carrying on regardless, slamming your head against a wall, isn't always right. That's why sometimes when contestants do hand me their armband, I'll congratulate them.

In this particular series, Anthea Turner was always at the back of every task, along with John Fashanu. I called them grandma and grandad. After day three I let all the others go in and hauled them out onto the parade square and stood them in front of me.

'Why are you two *always* at the fucking back.' I looked at Anthea: 'Do you want to hand your number in?'

'No, staff.'

'Listen, all you're doing is prolonging your suffering. It's inevitable. Fucking think about it; I'm doing you a favour here. Think about why you want to be here. You're hanging out of your fucking arse, you're always last. I think it's time for you.'

I said the same thing to John, who responded by standing to attention and bellowing back: 'I will improve, staff!'

We were all, what the *fuck*? While we were trying to compose ourselves, Anthea piped up again. 'Do you know what, staff, you're bang on. It was an absolute pleasure to be on this course, thank you for the experience.'

I don't think I could have given her more respect if she'd passed the course. Next day, John had gone. It turned out that he didn't improve. Not even close. Only one of them had been honest with themselves. She wasn't lying or bullshitting herself; instead she placed the problem squarely before her eyes, made an assessment of the situation and in doing so was able to appreciate how far she'd come. She emerged with a positive from a negative situation. In her eyes and mine she'd succeeded, and she could go out on a high.

Emilie

I was never one of those girls who believed in love at first sight. Then I met Anthony. Five minutes of talking to him in a bar and I was hooked. I remember that he turned to me at one point, after we'd been talking for hours that felt like seconds, and said, 'What do you want out of life?' Nobody had ever asked me that before. I was actually going out with someone else at the time. I'd been with this other guy for five and a half years, but for a while I'd had a feeling that it wasn't going anywhere. I left him that evening. I'm not sure that that night I had a clear sense I'd end up making a life with Anthony, but this first encounter with him had an amazing, clarifying effect. Whatever was going to happen in the future, I couldn't be with my old boyfriend anymore.

The next day, I needed to talk to my friend Emma, I think because I was surprised by the impact that my brief conversation with this strange, charismatic man had had on me. I'd never felt anything like that before.

'Do you believe in love at first sight?' I asked.

She just laughed at me. 'Emilie, that's the *worst* thing I've ever heard.'

'But that's how I feel.'

'Clearly, it's a feeling.'

And here we are now, sixteen years later.

The thing that struck me most about Anthony was that he was carefree, fun-loving. He wasn't one of those guys who were into designer labels. He didn't think about the clothes he put on, but somehow they always looked good on him. He seemed so happy in himself and didn't care what anybody else thought about him. I loved that about him. It's still true: he can read the most horrendous comments online and they fly straight over his head.

I'd never really thought about the phrase 'free spirit' before, and then when I met Anthony it just made sense. He sees the world in a completely different way to almost everyone else. For someone like me who's quite cautious by nature, it was so refreshing to look at life through his eyes. If someone says to me, 'Don't cross the line,' you don't need to worry, I'll do what I'm told. Anthony will smile and then hop over it. Being around him, it was so easy to get swept up in that. With Ant by my side, I couldn't care less about what other people think. Why would I?

It all comes from his childhood. At least, that's what I think. His experiences at that time carved out certain parts of his personality and made him a positive person. Very early on in life he made his mind up to better himself, and I don't think he's stopped since. His desire to push and push and push? That's from those early years. Since I've been with him, he's only ever stayed in the same job for a few years. A point always comes when he starts looking for the next thing. He's so relentless that sometimes I'll have to stop him and say, 'Your dreaming. It's making my head go fuzzy.'

There are days when he'll be off on one, talking about this or that, and I'll look him in the eyes and say, '*Calm down.* Why are you talking about our dream house? I thought we moved into that last year?'

'Yeah,' he'll say, 'I know, but …' And off he goes again.

It's because he's always trying to become a better person, to find some way to make our life better. It's one of the qualities that I love about him, and yet there are times when it can teeter a bit. They don't last long, but they're there. Luckily, over time, we've evolved a sort of creative tension between us. I like to plan our life, he seems to live it minute to minute. He pulls me forward and I pull him back.

LESSONS

Positive people are hungry to discover themselves. They know that there are no shortcuts and that it's only when you start to make the most of yourself that you'll also be making the most of life.

Once you've identified your strengths, make the most of them. They're a source of positive energy, so don't let them go to waste. No good ever came from hiding your talents away.

The people who love you will offer you constructive criticism. Make sure you listen to it.

Learn to treat your conscience as an important guide. Especially when that little voice is telling you things you don't want to hear.

Find your positive motivator. It's the single most important element in helping you survive negative situations unscathed.

If a weakness is stopping you from achieving something important to you, work ruthlessly to fix it. But remember that not all weaknesses need to be worked on.

CHAPTER 2

TEAR THE MOULD AWAY

THERE ARE SOME nights when my dreams are full of debris, those broken parts of my past that I realise will probably stay with me until the day I die. I'm not tortured by them, and yet they come back again and again. Recollections from the most gruelling moments of selection, scenes from combat – all of them return to me during the night. Most persistent of all are memories of what happened to me from the age of fifteen to twenty-one.

They're still so vivid to me, perhaps more so than those from any other part of my life. For everyone, it's an awkward stage. I was no different. You think you know everything; in reality you know fuck-all. Everything's in a whirl, and it's so hard to work out who you are and what you've been put on the planet to do. Even as you approach your third decade, you're still a baby.

They were my lonely years, the time when I was most by myself. I'd left home at fifteen and joined the military when I was sixteen. Although I got married at a very early age, I felt isolated. All my family were in France, and it seemed to me as if I was doing everything by myself – a weird and dislocating experience. If I fucked up, there was nobody around to be disappointed in me. If I succeeded, there was nobody to be proud of me. It didn't really matter what I did. My mind was full of questions that I could not find the answer to, and I was worried that there *were* no answers. Do I belong in the army? Do I belong in this relationship? Do I even belong in this country?

I was very well spoken back then and you could tell that I was an outsider. I had different ways about me. I was super-polite, super-respectful. When that wasn't reciprocated, I'd get surprised and hurt. People thought I was strange, as if there was something unsettling about my niceness. It made things hard to start with.

All you want to do when you're that age is fit in and be accepted. You don't want to stand out. On the one hand, you think you're too cool for your parents, and you want to go and conquer the world; on the other, you're probably mates with a bunch of immature kids who don't know what respect or success is. You end up on autopilot, taking the gentlest route possible.

You're so easily influenced when you're young, especially when you're entering an environment with a really strong identity like the Paras. I saw guys I'd become close to during training really change once they got their red berets.

I'd ask, 'Why are you doing that?'

Their response would always be a variation on, 'Waaay, it's what we do.'

'That's not you,' I'd reply. 'What are you being a knob for?'

'No,' they'd tell me, 'you're the one being a knob.'

Their idea of a good night was to put on fancy dress, head into town to savage a few pubs before coming back to the squadron bar to start drinking piss from pint glasses. If you wanted to be accepted, you had to endure endless nights out with men who all dressed the same – maroon squadron jumper with holes in it, ripped jeans and desert boots – playing endless games of pool and darts. Every fight, every bit of banter, every wrecked piece of pub furniture was greeted with the same moronic cry: 'Airborne! Airborne! Airborne!'

That was how soldiers passed their time. Between the Falklands and 2001 there was no regular theatre of operations. Going into town, beating each other up and drinking until they were sick was the only way they could get the aggression and anger out of their systems. I could get why they were behaving like that, but it just wasn't me.

Still, for a while I tried to fit in. I've talked in *First Man In* about how I matched them drink for drink. How I was stupid enough to want to earn their respect by fighting or throwing myself headfirst onto a dance floor carpeted with spilled booze and broken glass. How one drunken night I pissed all over the top deck of a bus.

Being a Para seeped into every aspect of my existence. When I was on duty, it dictated how I dressed, how I moved, what I said. When I was off duty, the same happened. When you're in that kind of all-encompassing environment, it's so hard to remind yourself that a world beyond the regiment even exists. I was surrounded by Paras and surrounded by the things they thought and believed. For a long time, when I had those moments of thinking, 'Fuck, is this what I *really* want, is this who I *really* am?' I'd end up convincing myself that it was me who had the problem. I could feel myself being pulled in two directions at once. Part of me wanted to be accepted by the others, another part was wary of losing too much of my personality or my values in the process.

As much as I wanted to get on, however, I found that the more I tried to remain myself, the more I was becoming alienated from the others. I knew that if I was willing to make the small amount of effort needed to become more like the other Paras, it would have opened up my path and I could have gone as far in that regiment as I wanted to – I'd been best recruit, and the best PT when I passed out of training, smashing it. And yet there was something inside me that was telling me to stop.

I was trying to figure out who I was while living in a different country to the one in which I'd spent most of my life. I was in the middle of an alien organisation that pretended to be like a family but in reality was anything but. And I was trapped in a relationship that I realised too late had been a mistake, but to which I was desperately clinging because it appeared to me to be the one element of normality I had left. There are kids who don't even have those rocks to balance on; how the hell are they supposed to find the space to sort their heads out?'

In those situations, the only way to grasp some sort of control is to rebel against everything. In your head there's a constant message saying: *nobody understands me; nobody even* wants *to understand me.* You forget at that age that the world *doesn't* revolve around you, so you get everything out of proportion. What you want more than anything is for the world to figure you out. It's only when that doesn't happen that you realise that it's hard labour that *only you can do.* Or, at least, the penny *should* drop. It doesn't always do so. There are people out there right now still waiting for the world to start working for them.

It's such an important developmental stage, one that's either going to make you or break you. After a while, I stopped trying to fit in. My attitude became: fuck the lot of you. I almost went out of my way to do things I knew would annoy them, stuff that would challenge their thinking and values.

I stopped going out on the lash with the lads. I'd just have a couple of beers and then slip off back home to my married quarters. Or I'd hit the gym – something I tried to do every night. I was a lifeguard, so I also had a job at the military garrison pool, which gave me a little second wage and some space. I think in retrospect I was probably a millennial before the term came into existence. If you'd put some avocado toast in front of me, I'd probably have been into it.

What was increasingly clear to everyone was that I didn't want to be around the other Paras, and they – quite understandably – didn't want to be around me. Things got bad. What I didn't realise at the time was that they were about to get worse.

NOT LONG AGO I was reading the paper and my attention was immediately drawn to a particular story. A soldier had been found dead in his barracks. Suicide. It had come out that he'd been bullied for years. For *years*. Instantly I was taken back to my own experiences in the army. My first thought was, *How is that* still *going on?* But then again, bullying was part of the fabric of our existence. Bullying for us was like water is to fish. It was inconceivable that things could be run without it.

In Signal troop, bullying was the mechanism the other Paras used to ensure conformity. It was a really cliquey group, and we had this reputation for being the cast-outs of the squadron. When lads from other troops saw what was going on, they were shocked. 'What the fuck are you *doing*?' Most of us who had come up in the troop didn't believe there was any other way of being. I think this was partly because the hierarchy were as much part of the problem as anyone. They knew what was taking place. In fact, they encouraged it. There was a real pack mentality. The people that got involved were hyenas with an almost uncanny ability to spot vulnerability or any divergence from the values they wanted to instil in us all. And when they came at you, they did it again, and again, and again. They were ferocious. Death by a thousand cuts.

There would always be a ringleader, and he'd be the one to identify the target. Then you'd see him and his pals talking and plotting among themselves. For a long time, it was something that I'd see happen to other people. Then, once I'd begun to alienate myself from the rest of the regiment, their attention turned to me. They'd all come back from a night on the piss, their breath heavy with stale beer and cigarette smoke, their eyes full of drunken malice, and they'd surround my bed in the accommodation block. Sometimes they tipped me out of it. Then they'd push my locker over, trash everything inside it. Just being cunts, really, all the while telling me, 'Middleton, you fucking need to mix in with the lads.'

I'd sit there, watching, knowing there was nothing I could *do* that could stop them, thinking to myself, *Don't tell me what to do, don't tell me what to do, don't tell me what to do.* Their behaviour only made me more determined to rebel against the sort of person they wanted me to become. To them, my individualism was a threat; it was an affront to their way of thinking.

The instigator in my troop was the troop sergeant, a little five foot six fucking rat called Squashie. He was a Cockney with a typical small-man syndrome, the sort of man who would just dig at people for the sheer pleasure of it. I'd overhear him talking in his office to other guys: 'I hear Middleton wants a place on this course, but I'm going to give it to you, and I want you to make sure he knows I've given it to you, not him. Make it clear.' Because of the place he occupied in the hierarchy, all the other soldiers would follow his lead – it was in their interests to do so, if only because if somebody else was being bullied, it meant they were safe. Temporarily, at least.

There was one morning when I walked into the stores room and found Squashie standing there, his little ratlike face full of malice, surrounded by a handful of his acolytes.

'Ah, Middleton, we've been waiting for you.'

'Ah, fucksake. What now?'

They'd attached a sledgehammer to a bungie rope. I looked around. It was obvious that there wasn't any way of getting out of the room without a fight, and I was nine stone wet, a seventeen-year-old streak of piss, so I'd have to endure whatever their bored, vindictive minds had prepared for me.

'Middleton. Stand there. We're going to swing this at you' – he pointed at the apparatus they'd built – 'and you've got to dodge it,' he finished, leering. The others sniggered.

'It's a fucking sledgehammer on the end of a bungie, you moron.'

'Just fucking *stand* there, Middleton.'

So they pinged it at me. I ducked and dodged. It was pathetic, as they'd gone to so much effort to set this thing up to torment me. Five, six minutes went by. But there was only a certain number of times I'd be able to evade it and they'd be bound to get lucky sooner rather than later. I really wasn't up for a smack in the face. The situation was getting out of hand, and I was beginning to think that maybe I'd have to do something to defend myself that I might regret later.

It only stopped when the door opened and a sergeant from another troop walked in. Everyone froze. For a moment that sergeant was so stunned by the scene he'd stumbled across that he could only stand there, blinking, trying to work out if his eyes were playing some kind of trick on him. Then his bewilderment gave way to anger.

'For fuck's *sake*. What the fuck are you all playing at? Fucking get to work. You fucking *degenerates*.'

As he did so he shot me a look, as if to say, 'You're better than this.' The rest of the dickheads looked like kids who'd been caught stealing sweets.

For me, it was an incredibly clarifying experience. That sergeant's reaction made me realise that I wasn't the only one thinking, 'This doesn't seem right.' I began to think that I needed to change troop, or perhaps do something even more dramatic. Was it time to bring my spell in the regiment to an end?

A couple of days later I spoke to the sergeant who'd broken everything up, and asked about joining his troop. He was still shocked by what he'd seen.

'No wonder you want out,' he said, shaking his head. 'Is that what goes on every day?'

'Yeah,' I said. 'I'm fucking sick of it.'

Over the following weeks we had a few more informal chats about me switching across. I was tempted, but by the time it became an actual possibility my mind was made up. I wanted to go in a totally different direction.

I WAS TWENTY-ONE when I quit the Paras, and my head was still all over the place. But it was overwhelmingly obvious that I was in a violently negative environment that was making me react in a violently negative way. I wanted to grow and learn and express myself. They just wanted to reduce me to their level. For a while I did end up behaving like them, and it was one of the most negative passages in my life. I hated myself for it.

It was different in the Marines and Special Forces. Partly because I had more life experience, and partly because their whole attitude is better. There was still the same rigid discipline in the Marines, but a far better culture, one that didn't ooze toxic testosterone. You didn't encounter so many of those lads who think they're everything because they've got a maroon beret – all you've done is complete a three-week course, so don't get too excited. Then, in the Special Forces, I could pretty much do what the fuck I wanted. The SBS was free of the rules, regulations, yes-sirring and button-polishing of the green army. We could wear civilian clothing and cut around camp with long hair and a beard. We were even able to pick the equipment we'd take to the battlefield.

What both the Marines and the SBS shared was a commitment to excellence. They prized becoming the best warrior you could possibly be over bullshit displays of bravado, and there was never a sense that individuality and ambition were regarded as threats. In the army, they'd want to smash you down if you stood out in any way. In the Marines and Special Forces, if you could do the job to the level they expected, they didn't care what you looked like, or if you could be a bit cocky on a night on the piss. There was an honesty about them. They weren't afraid of highlighting your weaknesses, but it was only ever because they wanted to help you overcome them.

'Fucking hell,' I remember thinking, a little while into the basic training for the Marines, '*this* is what it's supposed to be like.'

BUILD YOURSELF A POSITIVE HOME TO LIVE IN

Those bullies wouldn't try anything with me these days. As if they'd fucking dare. But reading articles about that sort of shit in the papers can still send a little shiver down my spine. Is that *still* going on? And when I talk to kids going through something similar, I feel this pulse of recognition. I can see the loneliness rising off them. Looking back on my own experiences, which still seem so close to me even now, the thing that's clearest to me is the importance of surrounding yourself with the right people, and of finding the right space in which you can do all of that growing up. I was still pretty innocent when I joined the Paras. I was inclined to trust people unquestioningly, and give them the benefit of the doubt. My experiences with them taught me that there are a lot of negative people out there. The world is full of them.

Now I know what I need to be positive. I need positive values, a positive mindset and positive people around me. I also need to ensure that I reciprocate all of that. If you hang around with negative people then you shouldn't be surprised if you end up behaving negatively yourself. By contrast, if the people around you are positive then you will be filled by their positive energy. You'll be bouncing off each other, rather than sucking away each other's will to live.

As you start to figure this out, you'll learn how to cut

more and more negative elements out of your life. You have to remember that we're all energy sources, capable of affecting anybody who comes into contact with us. I've found that I draw explosive amounts of energy from the experience of going on my tours, or in encounters with fans in the street. Going on stage, knowing that I'm going to be talking to a room filled with people who are all desperate to become the best versions of themselves, and that I can help them achieve this, is the most amazing feeling. These spaces radiate positivity, and I come away from them feeling charged-up and excited.

By contrast, if you stay in a negative environment for too long you'll become a negative person. Fact. It will suck the life out of you. It's the same with negative people. If you're surrounded by people who think and act negatively, then it's for fucking sure that you'll start doing the same.

It's up to you, really. Have a look around. Look at the environment you're in, the people you surround yourself with. Do they make you feel good about yourself? Do you feel as if they want you to become the best version of yourself? When you're with them, do you behave in a way that you're proud of?

If the answer to any of these questions is no, it's time for you to build a new, positive home for your life.

DON'T ENTERTAIN NEGATIVITY

I'm in such a positive place now that I can shy away from all negativity. This requires work and self-discipline on my part, and sometimes means giving up things that used to give me pleasure. But maintaining my positivity is so important to me that the sacrifice seems worthwhile. In fact, the benefits are so strong that it doesn't even seem like a sacrifice.

It's important to be alert to sources of negativity. Be aware of your environment. Challenge it. Ask yourself whether the chances are that if you go to see this person, or go to visit that place, you'll come back feeling more positive or negative than when you left the house. If the answer is that you'll be in a better state of mind, then brilliant. If you think you'll end up feeling worse, then don't hesitate to steer well the fuck away. I know that if you put me in a negative environment, I'm much more likely to start behaving in a negative way.

I've always had trouble when I've gone out. Once upon a time it was just standard alpha stuff: the other guy doesn't care who you are; they just want to prove they're the top man in that particular bar on that particular night. Now, though, with the profile I have, it's much more, 'Let's see how hard the SAS man really is.'

Take an average evening. I'll go to the pub with my mates. First thing people do is they stare. 'Oh, look, it's Ant

Middleton.' It's eight or nine o'clock, and the people there might have only had a couple of drinks. Everyone's friendly, they come up and ask for a photo or tell me they love *SAS: Who Dares Wins*. It's nice.

An hour or so later, their inhibitions have been washed away a bit by the booze, they become a little more familiar with you. Then, every time, no matter where I am, that's when the call comes up. 'Come on, Ant, let's have an arm wrestle.'

You try to be polite: 'No, you're all right, thanks. I'm fine, I'm just having a quiet drink with my friends.'

'Come on, mate!'

I fend them off, fend them off, but I'm already wondering if the evening is worth the hassle.

If I stay there for another hour it goes to the next level. I'll try to go to the toilet, and the same group who only a little bit earlier were asking for selfies and praising my shows now block my path. 'See if the SAS man can get past me.' They've had a few beers, they all think they're a foot taller than they actually are.

'Come on, dude.'

Or, as I'm walking to the toilet I'll feel something hit the back of my head, and when I turn round there'll be a bunch of lads sniggering to themselves, thinking they're clever because they've dipped a tissue into a pint and managed to lob it across the room.

I walk off. Slap. I get hit by another pellet. That's the moment when I think to myself: 'Right, I can either leave, or

I can go to the toilet and when I get back find out who the fuck threw that tissue at me.' Usually, by the time I've been for a slash I've calmed down. I can look at the little gaggle of idiots pissing themselves and walk past without taking the bait. It's not fun to have to say to your mates, 'Sorry, lads, that's my night over,' but I know that if I get into a fight, they'll feel duty bound to kick off too. Just as I know that the last thing my career, or my family, needs is for me to get caught up in a pub brawl.

So, as a way of avoiding unnecessary negativity, I don't really go to normal bars now. I always thought that people who went to private members' clubs were wankers. Now I understand. By the same token, I rarely get the train anymore.

It's fucking mad that me standing in the corner of a pub is also me placing myself in a vulnerable situation. But we are where we are. I know that when I started my career there were people waiting for me to fuck up. They thought I'd go out boozing and get into fights. They thought that I'd show 'the real Ant'. Well, I have. It's just that the real Ant is the person that I've defined, not the person that they *thought* I was.

At the same time, when I think of the responsibility I have, it makes me a better person. I know I'm a role model, I know I inspire people and that they listen to what I have to say. I have to practise what I preach. All it needs is one stray punch from me and everything I've built would be over. In seconds. I've already got a conviction for a violent offence.

If I get accused of even *hinting* at violence, I'll be looking at ABH.

I'm an ambassador for the Prince's Trust, a captain in the Royal Marine cadets. I'm doing what I love, helping to nurture the next generation; why would I want to throw that away? That's why I can't socialise in the way I used to anymore. Because the moment I do, I allow distractions into my life and lay myself open to the wrong sort of people.

That's my experience, but I guarantee that it's something everyone will recognise. We've all been in environments that we know in our heart of hearts are bad for us. It's not just that we don't like what we see; we don't like the way they make us feel. Going into that negative space means we end up behaving in ways we later regret, or it simply leaves us depressed or angry. If you can't flip a negative into a positive, then cut it away. There's nothing you can do, and it's better that you get it out of your life before it starts infecting you with its mould. I did this when I left the Paras. I hated the way they behaved, and I hated the way I behaved in response. I knew there was no way that I could single-handedly change the culture of an entire regiment, so I chose to remove myself entirely from that negative zone.

If you're in an office where you can tell there's a toxic atmosphere, grab your laptop and try to find a separate space in which to work. If someone challenges you, be honest about how you feel. Tell them that you're finding a colleague particularly hard to deal with, or that you're just having a bad day.

It's the same with other human beings. Ask yourself why you're feeling negative. Is it the situation you're in, or the people that you're around? It's simple; it's not rocket science.

If the way somebody is behaving towards you is making you argumentative or snappy, don't engage with it. Remove yourself from their presence. That's why people say that when anger kicks in you should go around the corner and take a minute to breathe deeply and calm down. When you return, everything is so much simpler and easier to deal with. And remember, nothing positive is going to come out of arguing with a negative person.

STAY AWAY FROM VAMPIRES

We all have them. People who only talk about *their* problems; those people where when you go for a drink with them an hour passes and you realise they haven't asked a single question about how you and your family are doing. These people behave as if they own you.

The great thing about being positive and building your own foundations is that when you do say 'No', because you don't owe anybody anything, these people won't have any comebacks.

I used to let everyone in, and yet I've learned the hard way that although it might seem like the right thing to do, it has its price. Ever since I got out of prison, when I meet people I ask myself: 'Are they going to help me become a better version of myself?' Their bank balance, their past, their job: all that is irrelevant. But if the answer to the question is 'No', I'll not entertain you. I'll still be polite and respectful, but I'll also be firm. No thank you.

I do something similar when I get offered business opportunities. As I'm being pitched to, I watch and I ask myself: Do they really believe in what they're doing? If things go wrong, will they turn around and start spraying blame about, or will they be the sort of people who will take responsibility and try to fix what has gone wrong?

There are people out there who are only interested in bringing you down to their level. They can't create positivity themselves, so they just try to suck away everybody else's. What a shitty place to find yourself in. Squashie was like that. He was so insecure about his own choices and habits that he couldn't bear the idea that I might be following my own interests or trying to better myself in my own way. When you see somebody doing things differently, you should be interested in that, as there might be something you can learn. Squashie felt threatened and acted accordingly. The sad thing was that there were others who helplessly allowed him to do that.

He was the sort of social vampire who *liked* being around bums. He was an idiot who had just enough about him that other idiots looked up to him. In that unit, he was the king of the fucking idiots. He used his position to create a circle of lame fools whom he could control, drawing on them as a resource to help them feel better. Negative people hate other humans being positive and will always try to attack them.

You have to remember that whatever people like Squashie might say about you, their behaviour towards you says far more about them than it does about you – you're irrelevant to them, just as they're really irrelevant to you. Don't be one of those people who forget that life should be about trying to pull yourself up, not tearing others down.

FIND YOUR MENTORS

You can only grow so much by yourself. I can pick up inspiration all the time from people from all walks of life. I might be on the street and I'll see a woman elegantly defuse an argument that's broken out. I'll think: that's something I can use myself in the future. Or I might see somebody conduct a deal and say to myself: fucking hell, that was really clever, I'll grab that. Being alert to your environment and the things we can learn from it is such a useful habit to develop. When you walk out of your door, don't just stare at the pavement in front of you. Keep your eyes open, be alive to the people around you and what they're doing. When you do that, you'll be living life on the front foot. It's such a positive, open way of being.

Most of all, however, I look to those closest to me. When I'm having a shit day and I feel down, I take a step back and think about the people that are most important to me in my life. There are about five. I only need to bring one of them to mind and it puts a smile on my face. Do you know why? I know that if everything came crumbling down around me, their positivity would lift me back up. It's not that they could lend me money or get me a job. It's their positive energy. I know that they want me to be more and more successful. Me doing well puts a smile on their faces. I know that I can rely on them to keep me headed in a positive direction.

If you're in the same position and you can't think of anybody who can put a smile on your face, then you've got the wrong people around you. The older I get, the more I understand how important it is to surround yourself with positive people. It's the quality that attracts me most to others. Emilie, for instance, or a guy called Mike Morris, a top businessman and friend who's become a kind of mentor to me.

I actually met him because I was doing a corporate event for his company. Normally these things are arranged by phone. But for one reason or another we couldn't quite connect, until I emailed to apologise for yet another failed attempt to arrange a call and told him I was in London. It turned out that he was 500 yards away from me.

Sometimes you get a particular energy off somebody – you can feel their positivity – and you connect instantly. That's what happened with us the first time we met. I don't think we mentioned his company a single time. Even now, three years later, I'm not even sure what his companies do.

The pressures I'd faced as an elite operator, and the pressures he was under as a top-end businessman, were, it turned out, really similar when you broke them down. We both have experience of being in phenomenally stressful environments where other people are relying on the decisions we make. We both know the loneliness that comes with that sort of responsibility. We both know the impulse that makes us seek it out.

We opened up immediately; there was no caginess. It was as if we recognised something in each other. Then we got extremely drunk. The trust he placed in me helped me understand that I was more than a soldier. It was so different to the relationships I'd formed during the military.

He's the person whose advice and wisdom I'll always seek, and I'll always get his read on new ideas and propositions. In turn, I can help him when he's facing situations where he's unsure about what step to take next. It's value for value – we're both contributing as much as we're taking. Together, we create an energy that's greater than either of us can generate on our own. We've each seen the other when we've been at our most vulnerable. To begin with, it felt as if I was taking a risk opening up to him. Now I realise it's one of the best things I could have done. Every time I see him I come away feeling more positive, as if his energy supercharges my batteries.

He's a similar height to me – put a beard on him and you'd probably say we're related. But the people you surround yourself with don't always need to be the same as you. In fact, you need different perspectives and qualities. Emilie and I share a lot of values, but we're like chalk and cheese in our ultimate outlook. I like to go out and dive into risky situations. Emilie wants to create a world in which risk has been removed. She wants to build a stable empire where everything is planned, I like to take things as they come. I feel as if we complement each other. Together we are more than the sum of our parts.

Emilie is another person I see as a role model. She's the key to who I am and has provided the foundation for everything I've ever achieved. If I didn't have Emilie, I'm not sure I'd even want to *start* guessing where I'd be. I know how much she's sacrificed so that I can go out there and live the life I have. In return, she loves me being the protector, the provider. She thrives off bringing up our kids and works herself to the bone to give them everything she can. She loves being a mum, seeing her children smile and laugh and learn. If she wanted to go off and do something different, I'd support her 100 per cent, but for the moment she's where she wants to be.

We're the epitome of a traditional family: husband, wife and kids. I know that maybe it's not so fashionable these days, that some people are even questioning what a family should look like. That's fine, that's their opinion. This is just what works for us. What's important is that we've always been honest with each other about what we both want. The worst thing either of us could do would be to hold on to a resentment.

Emilie and Mike are the sort of people I wish I'd had around me all those years ago when I felt so adrift. I know that they'd have provided the support I was so desperate for, just as they'd also have told me when I was behaving in a way that let myself down.

It all comes down to a simple equation: if the people around you aren't working for you, they'll be working against you.

NEGATIVITY IS LIKE A MOULD

Negativity is like a mould. As soon as it starts growing on you, you've got to cut it off. If someone's coming to you, draining the life out of you, stopping you getting where you need to be, cut them out. At the very least, you have to find a way of stopping that mould spreading.

In my last book, *The Fear Bubble*, I talked about how I had to cut my brother Dan out of my life. I hated doing that, but I know that it was a decision that was best for both of us. And it's worked out. Me sending him that message has led to him turning things around. The positive elements in his life now outweigh the negative. In fact, he's actually living with us at the moment. Our relationship has entered a completely new phase.

My experiences mean that I'm very quick to spot people in similar situations. For instance, my wife had this friend. Every time Emilie came back home after seeing her she'd be so down and depressed I could barely recognise her. I'd say, 'Have you been round so and so's?' And she'd be like, 'Yes, how did you know?' Nine times out of ten, if you cut out that one person, things improve almost immediately. That's certainly what Emilie discovered when she gently pulled away from that friend and eventually stopped seeing her altogether.

A similar thing happens with families. Some children are born into negative environments and it can seep into them. They grow up thinking that everything is against them, that they can't do this, that they're not capable of doing that. You hear all this talk about children suffering from stress and anxiety at the ages of ten, eleven. Sure, there are some extreme cases – and I'm not talking about that other scale, where kids have been abused or have deep-rooted psychological issues – but mostly it's because that child is living with a negative individual, the sort of person who can drain the energy out of you, the one who's not having a bad day, or a bad week, they're just riddled with negativity. Living with someone like that, the poor child is trapped in a negative bubble.

I remember one night on my last tour during the Q&A section, a woman put her hand up and asked me, 'How can I make my child more positive? He's just so negative at the moment.'

The answer came to me straight away. I said, 'You're asking the wrong question. The question should be, "Why is that child negative?" It's either the situation he's in, or it's somebody close to them. Who is negative in your family?'

Silence. Suddenly I saw that she'd become overwhelmed by emotion, and that something was stopping her from speaking. You could tell that *she* was the person exerting a negative influence on her boy – and she knew it. It was written all over her face. She didn't need to say a word.

The most extreme response – cutting that person out of your life, like I did with my brother Dan – is always the most effective. But I'd be lying if I said it was always straightforward or even possible to extricate yourself from a family situation just like that. The trick is to make sure that you establish which elements of the situation you can control, and which you can't. Focus on what you can fix, and don't let what's out of your grasp weigh down on you. If you're aware that your mother is a negative influence, then that's half the battle won. You can't necessarily stop her behaving in a way that upsets you, but you can limit the time you spend with her. You can't stop her saying hurtful things, but you can tell yourself that she's only doing this because she's a negative person.

DEAD-END THINKING

There are some people who are purely negative. They never have a good word to say about anyone or anything, and they actually seem to prefer finding problems to finding solutions. Sometimes it can feel as if they're actively trying to make the world a worse place. You should do everything you can to avoid them. They're poison when it comes to personal relationships and can have an outsized impact in a team environment.

One of the shows I'm most proud of working on is *Escape*. The premise was that each episode was loosely based on a real-life disaster. In the last episode of the programme, we were re-creating a plane crash on a glacier. We ended up making a tank out of two jet skis and the front of the plane, which we'd cut off to provide us with protection against the wind. There was one guy from Manchester, maybe the most annoying person I've ever met. In his view, we didn't need that visor because he didn't think we'd be out and about on our bastardised vehicle for very long. And he wasn't afraid of telling us, even when I tried to explain to him that there was a chance that we could be travelling for ages without finding anything. We had enough petrol for nearly twenty miles and we wanted to get the max out of that. But there was no chance we'd be able to drive around in this environment, the largest glacier in Europe, with its ice-cold winds, without some sort of protection. Our faces and hands would freeze off.

His only response to this was to complain and complain, and then complain some more. It was too cold and too hard, and he didn't think what we were doing was necessary. There was one morning when we were trying to saw the front of the plane off when he chirped up in his nasal voice: 'I'm sleeping in here!' 'Fine, but how else do you think we're going to get out of here!'

He'd list all the things that *could* happen to us when we got our buggy up, and his conclusion was always the same. The fact that something might happen was reason enough to not try at all. He objected to every single thing we wanted to build. Whenever he was presented with a solution, he found a problem. When someone else in the team addressed the issue, he'd simply find another. You could quickly see the impact his negativity was having on everybody around him. It left them deflated, unsure of themselves. They were all quite prepared to consider worst-case scenarios, but this was different. It seemed that he got more pleasure from spotting problems than he did from identifying fixes to them. He was like a hose, spraying everything and everyone around him with his negativity, a perfect example of how, ultimately, negative thinking is dead-end thinking. It gets you nowhere and instead leaves you trapped.

That's how powerful negativity is: it can take down a whole team.

Emilie

The question I always get, *always*, when it comes to Anthony is: 'Is he really that positive? Isn't it bullshit? He can't be as happy as that all the time.'

I think my answer always comes as a disappointment. I know that what people want me to say is that as soon as the front door closes and he's out of sight of the cameras, he turns into a monster. The truth is quite different. He's *irritatingly* positive.

He never wallows. Most people have days where they give off a vibe that basically says: 'Don't come anywhere near me.' You never get that with Anthony. He just doesn't do it. I don't know how, but he doesn't. Ever. It's as if he doesn't have that mechanism inside him.

I love his attitude to life. It's inspiring and fun, but there are times when it irritates me. Anything you throw at him, *anything*, he'll always flip it into a positive, no matter how overwhelming the situation.

There have been moments when I've had to say, 'It's not going to be fine, though, is it?' And he's looked back at me as if *I'm* the mad one. Sometimes he'll tell me that I'm negative. My first response to that is usually, 'Stick your negativity … I'm not negative, I'm a realist. These are the facts, this is what's happening right now.'

In the days before his sentencing, he was convinced he'd either get a tiny stretch, or maybe even avoid prison altogether. I was a mess of nerves, because I could see that him going away like that had the potential to throw a bomb into our life. He was different. 'It'll be fine. It'll be fine.' He kept on saying that.

Then he got fourteen months.

'It really isn't going to be fine though, is it? You're going to prison. What am I going to do? We've got two children.'

'Yeah, but you don't need to tell the kids, they're not old enough to take it in. And it's a chance to turn my life around. This is actually a good thing for me.'

Oh my God. What can you do with that?

His positivity rubs off on you. Lots of people say that after spending time with him they come away feeling energised. I know how they feel. But I think his positivity has had a more subtle effect on me. One of the odd things about being with Anthony is that I notice negative people around me in a way I would never have before. It's the cumulative result of being around someone so relentlessly upbeat. So now if somebody is giving off that vibe, I know I can't be around them, because I know the effect it will have on me. Ten minutes in their company and I'll be absolutely exhausted, like I've run a marathon.

There are people I love, who I know are good people, but I know that I have to be careful about limiting my exposure to them, because they'll drain my energy. I've realised that I'd rather be with my children, in my home, enjoying their company, than hanging around with the kind of people who spend their days sitting in coffee shops moaning about others. Surely there's more to life than that?

LESSONS

If you're in a negative environment, get out of there. No good will come of staying put. All you'll be doing is absorbing negativity yourself.

We're all energy sources. Some people radiate positive energy, others blast out negativity. Make sure you surround yourself with the most positive individuals you can.

Stay away from vampires. When you meet someone, ask yourself if they're really interested in helping you become the best possible version of yourself, or whether they want to bring you down to their level.

Grab inspiration from positive people whenever you can. It doesn't matter if they're your wife, or somebody you've only seen from across a room. Why deprive yourself of the chance to add another positive tool to your armoury?

Other people's negativity is their problem, not yours. Don't let them load you up with their bad vibes.

CHAPTER 3

KILL THEM WITH KINDNESS

OCTOBER 2007. HELMAND Province, Afghanistan. It was hot, the sun hammering down on us. The sort of day when it's hard to keep your spirits up. You just want to be back at base, feet up, drinking something cool. Instead, you're struggling around the landscape, encased in body armour, for what seems like hours on end. *Fucking* Taliban, *fucking* patrols, *fucking* sweat pouring down the back of my neck, *fucking* Afghan.

All of us were carrying loads of twenty-two kilos, sometimes more – the Taliban used to laugh at us, calling us camels and tortoises. To them, cutting about in flowing robes, we looked like clumsy fools. Every man was dragging along with them front and back plates (and I had an Israeli cop vest for good measure), helmet, webbing, personal weapons, ammunition, radios and six litres of water – in that weather we needed a *lot* of water. You don't really feel it when you walk out of the gate. You do five hours in. *Fucking* Taliban, *fucking* patrols, *fucking* sweat pouring down the back of my neck, *fucking* Afghan.

At the time I was a section commander, in command of seven other Marines. Our regiment was based in our Forward Operational Base (FOB), Sangin District Command. Each unit was responsible of an Area of Operations (AO) of about seven square miles. It would then get broken down still further for patrols – we'd be out for twelve, fourteen hours a day. These patrols were to make sure that the villages weren't being infiltrated by the Taliban, or any other terrorist entity. And if there was anyone hostile in the area, we wanted to persuade the villagers to let us know.

Mostly we did this by knocking on the doors of the compounds they lived in. Some people were willing to open up, others weren't. Sometimes those in the second category found their door being knocked down very soon after they'd said the word 'No'. I wasn't much of a fan of this approach; people don't generally tend to be that chatty when you've smashed their front door off its hinges.

But most of the time we got on well with the villagers. You're there for six months, going past their houses every day. Unless you're a real dick, you build a rapport with them. We'd nod acknowledgement of each other's presence in the street, stop to shoot the breeze when they looked up for it (as much as you can when neither party knows more than a few words in the other's language) and knew when to leave them alone if they were busy.

They could be wary at times, which when you think of the nation's history was hardly a surprise. For much of the

1980s the country was torn apart by a vicious war with the Soviet Union, who had invaded in 1979. That was followed by the grim, repressive rule of the Taliban, and then after 9/11 the British and Americans showed up. In between that were all sorts of squabbles between the local warlords, who were forever trying to assert their power. It was easy to see why the normal citizens would be left bewildered by the constant violence; all they wanted to do was to be able to get on with their lives in peace.

I never felt as if we were in Afghanistan as an occupying force. As I saw it, we were there to protect those villagers. We were providing a service to them. At the same time, I was always conscious that there was a line that had to be preserved. We had to make sure we looked menacing enough to act as a deterrent. And it was important that we never let our professionalism lapse, even for a second. I'd tell my patrol that they could not allow the locals to click on that they were tired or struggling – easier said than done when we were out for fourteen hours at a time on patrol. Every single day. It was brutal.

I think in a way it was easier for me as a section commander. I always had something to keep my mind occupied: checking on the other seven men with me – making sure they were all right, that their kit was fine – or planning for the next patrol. Also, I loved what I was doing; I was always hyped for it.

I loved it, even though there could sometimes be something quite depressing about patrolling the same patch of territory again and again and again. Someone else had fought and died to win it for our side. And somebody else, far away from the heat and dust, would decide, at some point in the future, that it was no longer strategically necessary that we should hold these villages. Then we'd withdraw. We were aware that in some broad sense we were making a meaningful contribution to the war effort, but we rarely saw any real results.

It was only later on, when I was going on special operations, that I ever got the feeling I was making a *personal* difference. If you kill an IED facilitator, for instance, then somebody else, without his experience or knowledge or authority, is going to have to step into his shoes. It might mean a month, or more, of quiet. Which means a month, or more, when British soldiers don't get blown up. Seeing the positive consequences of the operations you're going out on really underscores the importance of what you're doing.

We never got that very much when we were patrolling like this; if I wanted to feel a bit of positivity about what we were doing, then I'd have to generate it myself.

YOU KNEW WHEN there were Taliban around, even before you'd got an intelligence report. Whole villages would just shut down, their inhabitants warned by the insurgents that if any of them were caught talking to us, they'd be dealt with. The streets would be empty except for a couple of stray dogs. It was like there was a shift in atmospheric pressure.

Over the previous days word had come that that there had been sightings of men in the area who were potentially hostile, so our patrol felt that bit more purposeful. There was always an extra layer of tension when you knew that the enemy was close by, which added to the exhaustion that came with being out there for such a long time.

The Afghan countryside was beautiful in its own way, but it could be unforgiving. The territory we were patrolling was full of steep inclines that seemed to sap every ounce of energy from you as you struggled to the top. Sometimes, as you walked through mile after mile of empty countryside, putting one tired foot in front of the other, it could seem as if the only things left on the planet were sand, rocks, little spiny plants – and your patrol. Occasionally you'd see footprints, which provided a short diversion as we tried to establish whether they were a sign that the Taliban were moving around the area, or if we'd just come across the tracks of a goat-herder.

The physical effort was matched by the mental energy you expended. Sangin was a dangerous place to be at the best of times, especially during the days when there was renewed activity. We all had to be on constant alert, eyes scanning the scrubby landscape around us, ears straining to pick up any unusual noises. The threat of ambushes and potshots taken at us from deserted buildings was one thing, the danger posed by IEDs was something else entirely. The idea that an innocuous patch of dirt in the road or a boy walking towards you pushing a trolley might conceal a weapon capable of tearing you and anyone around you into bloody scraps ate away at you constantly. We were up against an enemy who was playing by completely different rules.

It was late morning now, nearly midday. My body heat was soaring as the scorching sun climbed higher into the sky, and my feet sank an inch into the dunes with every stride. It wasn't long before my neck and back were pouring sweat and my mouth felt drier than the desert itself. I was struggling to work out if I'd ever felt as drained or hot as this at any point in my life.

I took a gulp of warm water from my canteen and looked up. Ahead of me were dunes and mountains, to my right nothing but hazy hot air and the horizon. And a lone tree. Just behind that was a fairly big compound, which stood on the edge of a small village. This would be our first port of call.

I strode over, my interpreter a couple of paces behind, and knocked on the door.

The head of the household, a guy in his fifties with a long beard, wearing a dark brownish red turban and dishdash, opened the thick door a couple of inches and poked his head out.

Peering past him I could see the smoke from cooking fires and a few kids running helter-skelter about the compound's courtyard. It was a typical arrangement: sunbaked bricks, washing hanging on lines, the tempting smell of bread baking. Domestic life carrying on as it always did, whatever else was happening in the country around it.

The old guy denied having seen any enemy activity, but there was something sheepish about him, as if he knew far more than he was willing to let on. His eyes wouldn't meet mine, and his knuckles were white where he was anxiously gripping the door.

Speaking through the interpreter again I explained why we were on patrol, and asked if there was any chance we could come in – even for just a couple of minutes – for a quick chat. 'No!' He refused, more forcefully this time – although I could tell it was worry, not aggression driving his reaction. There was something about his manner that made me want to press him a bit more. I didn't even need the translation – it was written all over his lined, craggy face. We tried a third time, at which point he slammed the door in my face. It was clear I'd need to try another way of persuading him.

Just before we'd been posted, we'd been given crash cards to help us learn a bit of Pashto, one of the two official languages of Afghanistan. And the more we communicated with the locals and immersed ourselves in their culture once we got there, the more we picked up. I didn't always know the precise meaning of the words and phrases, but you could tell from watching the speakers' faces whether they were negative or positive sentiments, and gradually get a bit more confident employing them yourself.

I'd done the same in France. The more you commit to it, the easier it becomes. If you try to push back against the culture, or just ignore it, you won't fit in or pick things up as quickly. There are a million tiny cues and packets of information that you'll never learn in a classroom. You simply have to be there. I'll tell anyone thinking about travelling abroad that if you don't respect the culture or the laws of the land you're heading to, don't bother. What's the point of going to Spain if you're going to sit drinking Boddingtons and eating an English breakfast in a pub showing endless re-runs of *Only Fools and Horses*? Approach it like that, and it just becomes a hot Margate.

I've always loved the process of understanding people so you can get on with them. It's exciting to me to be surrounded by people who look at the world in a completely different way to me, and you had a really strong sense in Afghanistan of an ancient society that had evolved over the centuries. Moving to France when I was a kid had been a culture shock; this, however, was on a whole different level. There were all sorts of elaborate rituals and customs that might at first appear difficult to follow, and yet steadily – the more you were exposed to them – they began to make sense. I felt as if I was learning every day, and now one of the things I'd picked up gave me a little bit of inspiration. Suddenly I realised how I could persuade the old Afghan to invite us in.

We knocked on the door again and reiterated how important it was that we talk to him without being watched. I said that we understood that the presence of militants in the area was unnerving. As we spoke, I looked him in the eye, made a big play of being able to smell something delicious, and said, '*Doday*', the word for bread in Pashto.

'Yes,' he said, still looking wary.

'Can we nip in, grab a bit of that delicious bread? Then we'll be on our way. We've been out on patrol for hours, we're all a bit hungry.'

This was something that I knew he could not refuse. One of the things about the Afghan villagers is that they're bound by a two-thousand-year-old tradition of hospitality called *Pashtunwali*. If somebody, even if they're a stranger, comes to you asking for help, or food, or shelter, you have to offer it to them. To do otherwise would be a source of great shame. That's why so many of the compounds had outhouses – in case they needed to house unexpected guests.

For a moment he seemed taken aback. I think he was surprised we'd asked for help like that. Then he looked from me to the interpreter and back to me again, took a step back and beckoned my team in. Seconds later there were eight of us inside the compound. While I did the hearts and mind stuff, along with three others from the section, the other fire team hoisted themselves up to the roof, just to make sure they could keep a discreet watch on everything that was happening in the surrounding area. If there were Taliban lurking around, I didn't want to let them catch us on the hop.

The courtyard inside the compound was maybe ten metres square. It was filled with goats, a big dog on a lead who started barking at us the moment he spotted us and a little gang of children who stopped whatever game they'd been playing and stared at us, mouths open wide.

When I saw the kids I slung my weapon, took my helmet off and approached them. There were maybe five of them. I got down on my knees and very gently put my hand out, said '*Salaam*', asked them how they were (in the process using all of the Pashto I'd picked up over the past few months, which wasn't that much) and watched as they put their hands on mine.

Straight away you could see that their father, the man who only seconds previously had been riddled with anxiety, was smiling and relaxed. He'd seen me for what I was – a dad just like him. It was clear to him I didn't have any ulterior motive, I was just happy to play with his children, a brief snatch of normality and innocence amid the fear and tension of the tour.

At that point he brought over a huge piece of bread, fresh from the upside-down dish it had been cooked on, and handed it round, each of us breaking off a chunk then passing it on to the next man. It was good sitting there in that compound in the middle of a warzone, eating delicious fresh bread with this cagey old Pashtun. It sounds like a bit of a cliché, but I stopped being a soldier and he stopped being an Afghani villager. We were just two men sharing a meal.

A few minutes of companionable eating and playing with the children – who were all trying my helmet on and giggling – passed before we started talking again. By this time barriers had been broken down, and he'd come to understand that we were here *for* him, and that all we wanted to do was ensure that he and his children were protected.

During the time we'd been eating the bread I tried to put myself in his shoes and asked myself: what would I be worried about if I was in his position? I don't really go in for that very scientific way of 'reading' people. But I'm very aware of other people and their surroundings and what's going on in their life. Even to take on 10 to 20 per cent of their mindset really helps you to think a bit more like them, and that in turn helps form a connection with them. That's as true of simple Pashtun tribesmen as it is billionaire entrepreneurs. I probably go a bit further than most people in this respect. I try to get to the point where I actually *feel* the pressure they're under. You won't always get everything absolutely right, but you'll always be able to strike a chord with one element. Even better if you can find five, but one is a start; people can see that you're authentic. Ultimately, you can't force relationships; you have to build them. If there's no trust there, it's probably not going to work.

If the Taliban had caught him with me, or even if they'd just clocked that we'd spent a bit longer than usual in his compound, he'd have been killed. They had people watching all the time – it was one of the many ways they ensured that the villagers lived in permanent fear. I explained that we were well aware that the mere fact of our presence put him at risk, but that we'd pay a visit to every compound in the area, and from then on do our patrols in a way that avoided setting any patterns, so that the Taliban wouldn't have any reason to single him out.

Don't worry, I assured him, we can give you a telephone. At the slightest hint of trouble all you need to do is call our interpreter, and we'll come over and look after you. This seemed to set his mind at rest. He'd already become far less tense, but now he looked positively relaxed. Ten minutes later the tea came out. And once we'd drunk that he started holding my hand as we spoke – a Pashtun sign of respect. He was cheerful and friendly now; it almost got to the point where it seemed he didn't want us to go. Cup of tea followed cup of tea. I think we'd all had about ten cups by the time we finally left.

He was also far more expansive than he'd been before. 'Yes,' he said, 'your intelligence is right. The night before, a group of Taliban came through.' Picking up enthusiasm, he told us everything he'd seen and heard. What had been a speculative visit was beginning to yield valuable intelligence.

He'd let his guard down. Unfortunately, so did I. I was so into the idea of playing the favoured guest that when he took a tub out from the folds of his dishdash and spread some of the dark brown paste inside his gums, I asked him what it was.

'Oh, tobacco,' he said smiling.

'Great! Give us some then.'

I probably should have known something was up when he started laughing. I looked to the interpreter – his face gave nothing away. I wasn't confident it was tobacco, or at least not *just* tobacco, but I reckoned that since it was clearly something that he took every day, there probably wasn't much to fear.

Five more minutes of warm chat followed, before we left to pay our respects to the rest of the village. I still had this little pad of 'tobacco' secreted inside my mouth as we carried on with the patrol. It was only about ten minutes later that I thought that maybe something was a bit weird about it. First I felt a bit nauseous, so I spat the paste out. Not long after that I realised how light-headed I was, then I began to feel really fucking strange. I walked along, giggling to myself about the situation – remembering the cannabis plants that grow in profusion all across the country. Yeah, I thought to myself drowsily, the words not quite linking together into normal sentences, that's what I've done. In my desire to show respect to this family, I'd consumed something that probably wasn't very wise at all.

As I pushed on, that feeling of spaciness that had come over me started to wear off, though not disappearing completely. I felt relieved that none of the other Marines had seen me jam that paste into my mouth. There obviously would have been a way to explain to my commanding officer how it was that I'd left our base a warrior, and come back a stoned hippie, but, Jesus, I was in no fucking state to come up with anything right now.

BE A SOCIALITE

When Emilie's parents first met me they thought that my politeness and positivity were a front. They were convinced that at some point I'd drop all that and show my true colours. I married Emilie two years later, and it wasn't until eight years after that that her dad Phil came up to me one day and said, 'When you first stepped through the door I thought that your politeness would wear off. I've known you for a decade now and it's still there. That part of you is *you.*'

They know now that my natural way of being is sincere. There's no hidden agenda – it's who I am. They see me with my friends, or the way I am around my children, and know that this is me.

You can put me in a room with anybody and I bet we'd get along. Being able to socialise with people, whether they're a CEO you're doing a multi-million-pound deal with or the most humble beggar in the street, is a crucial life skill.

To my mind it's up there with any other accomplishment you might want to name. When you know how to socialise and connect with other people, you'll find that opportunities will present themselves.

Being polite and respectful are values that have been instilled in me from childhood. Manners will get you somewhere rather than nowhere. This is what I tell my own kids: say please and thank you, open doors for women, offer to help clean up after dinner. People think life skills are things like being able to read and write. No, that's just education. Life skills start from the moment you hold that child in your arms for the first time. Because they'll be watching what *you* do; how you act will have such a huge impact on the development of their personalities.

Imagine two women going for a job. One is almost a genius – she's got more degrees than I've had hot dinners – but she can't look the interviewer in the eye. The other one might not know as much as the woman with all the degrees, perhaps she didn't even go to university, but she's got the sort of social skills that helps her figure life out. She's open and confident and polite. Nine times out of ten you'll go for the person who can look you in the eye while you're talking to them.

I feel good when I can make people smile, so I do everything I can to make sure that anybody whom I meet goes away thinking, 'Yeah, Ant seems like a good guy.' I'll laugh and joke with waiters, and always thank them for everything they've done for me. I'll listen to people's stories and ask questions about their lives. If you go around exuding positivity, you'll very soon find that positivity bouncing back at you. The nicer you are to people, the nicer they are back to you. It sounds obvious, but people get so wrapped up in the fact that they're late for their meeting, or that their morning has got off to a bad start, that they forget.

These sorts of interactions won't just make your life easier, although I guarantee that you'll get served quicker in restaurants! They'll also leave you with a warm glow. Because positivity isn't a limited resource; being kind and friendly is like an engine that creates more of the same. Do people favours, pay them compliments, make them feel good about themselves. It's nice to be nice. It also becomes a habit. Try to make every encounter you have with others a positive one. The more you do it, the more it'll be like a reflex. It'll become your natural reaction to meeting people. You'll feel at ease, and you'll help others feel comfortable around you.

WEAR THE HAPPY MASK

Don't get me wrong. I don't always *feel* positive. Like everyone I have highs and lows. Like everyone I can get annoyed by bad traffic or a tax bill or whatever. But I don't think it's fair to unload that negativity on other people. I'm a positive person – so why would I change who I really am because of a situation? I don't want to let that situation dictate how I behave and feel.

If you're feeling snappy or antagonistic to other people, ask yourself why. For me it could be that I've dropped my daughter off late at school, and I hate being late, hate being that sort of father. In that instance, when I've thought it over for a few seconds, I realise very quickly that there's nothing I can do about it – it's done, in the past – so I don't worry about it anymore. Your friends and family, even strangers you meet, they've all got plenty of stresses and strains in their lives. Why add to them by burdening them with your negative thoughts?

That's why I love going to America, where, in my experience, every interaction I have with a waiter or taxi driver or shopworker is so positive that it becomes infectious. When I had that encounter with the Afghan elder I was tired, hot and beginning to feel irritable. If I'd let any of that creep out it would have made it far harder to form a bond with him. I wore a happy mask – and it worked for me and for him.

WALK A MILE IN THEIR SHOES

You can't just live in your own head. Be curious about what's going on inside other people's minds. I made a connection with that Afghan elder because I was able to see the situation from his perspective. I knew that he was anxious about the possibility that the Taliban might spot that he was helping us, so I reassured him.

If you take the time to try to imagine what other people might be feeling – what their own fears, or hopes, or expectations are – it will make forming a positive connection with them and winning their trust so much easier. It's also a valuable tool in what should be an ongoing progress: self-reflection. Spending a bit of time in another person's shoes gives you that space you need to be objective about your own behaviour. It means you can get a sense of how you're coming across, and how your own actions impact on other people.

BE A LOVER, NOT A FIGHTER

I enjoy breaking people's fronts down. And positivity is an amazing tool with which to do that. I try to avoid giving people the opportunity to be negative towards me, because I don't deal well with confrontation. I know what I'm capable of in those situations, and I want at all costs to avoid letting the negative side of my character out. That negative part of me is *extremely* negative.

These days, I don't take the bait. Instead, when people have a go at me, I just kill them with kindness. Being nice to people who are determined to be unpleasant to you knocks them off balance. It's the last thing that sort of person expects, and they're not prepared for it. They wanted a fight, and what they got instead was a hug. You keep the moral high ground, and you also get to set the terms of that encounter.

I get the chance to put this theory into practice more often than I'd like these days. Ninety-nine per cent of the people I meet are really nice. Then you've got that tiny minority who get in my face, trying to provoke me: 'You're a sell-out. You shouldn't be out there exposing yourself on TV, talking about the Special Forces. How dare you make money off the back of it?'

What they expect is for me to go, 'Fuck you,' and kick off.

Instead, I'll ask, as calmly and politely as possible, 'Well, why do you think that?'

You can instantly see them deflate a bit. They'll try again, but with less conviction: 'You shouldn't be doing it.'

Then I say, 'Mate, I've got family to feed. I appreciate your opinion, but the military doesn't pay my bills or put a roof over my family's head. This is how I make ends meet.'

They're expecting the chief instructor, but what they get instead is a human being. I get the same on social media, and I do exactly the same: I douse them with positivity.

One of the things that people don't realise is that one of the reasons that I'm so positive is that I'm a fighter of negativity. I don't look at negative people and think, 'What an arsehole.' What I'm wondering is, 'What's going on in their heads? What are they feeling to be so riddled with negativity?'

I've always wanted to help people. Some people take trolling really, really bad, but I see it as an opportunity. When I get some keyboard warrior coming after me, I'm like, 'Right, let's see what we can do here!' I'll either laugh at it, or I'll kill them with kindness. I've also learned that when you're confronted with negativity, the most effective thing you can do is fight back with positivity.

I was really nervous ahead of my second speaking tour. It was a brand-new show I'd written myself that I was performing in front of two to three thousand people at a time. The very first night was in Ipswich, of all places. I stepped out into the lights, looked up at this huge sea of faces, and got cracking. Everything seemed to go well. The audience were enjoying it, my nerves had died away, and as the interval approached I found that I was relaxing into the night. I brought the first half to a close by telling the audience that the next segment would be about my adventures on Mount Everest, and warned them not to get too drunk.

As I walked off to a load of applause, my attention focused on this one guy who was slumped in his chair in the front row. While everyone around him, including his wife, was clapping, he had his arms defiantly crossed and was looking at me as if to say, 'Who's this prick?' He was doing everything he could, short of walking out, to show that he wished he could be anywhere in the world but here. He was fuming. I have no idea why.

I just started laughing to myself as I strode off backstage. I was thinking, 'Wow, that guy has just paid to come and see me. His wife's having a great time, and all he wants to do is make faces at me from his front-row seat. That's fucking brilliant.' His reaction could have engulfed me with negativity, making me think that all my effort had been wasted, that the evening was a disaster. A lot of people, when they're confronted with negativity, absorb that negativity and it becomes their own. Instead, it set me up to go and smash the rest of the tour. Every time I thought about it, just the image of him with his gorilla arms crossed beneath his angry face, it made me smile. I don't know what it was: maybe his missus had forced him to go, or maybe something I'd said had rung a bit of a bell – had been a bit too close to the bone for him. He stayed the same during the second half. It was a challenge. I wanted to disarm him, to try to work out why he was behaving so negatively towards somebody he didn't even know.

Every night, I found myself looking for someone else like that. I wasn't interested in those people who were enjoying themselves. I wanted haters, negative people, to be sitting in the audience, because they're the ones in greatest need of that positive message. I wanted to show them that in the past I too have thought negatively – and it got me nowhere. I wanted to inspire them to maybe try a different way of thinking. The last thing they need is for me to throw out more negativity. What might help them, though, is being killed with kindness.

NO BLANK CHEQUES

The reactions we got from the locals in Afghanistan varied immensely. Sometimes they were standoffish and anxious, sometimes they were almost too friendly. It could be hard to calibrate your reactions – on the one hand, we wanted to be seen as a warm presence; on the other, we were soldiers operating in a hostile environment.

A lot of the guys decided the best thing was to operate all day every day with a poker face. But I'm so positive and curious about others that I couldn't restrict myself to a one-dimensional role like that. At the same time, I knew that there had to be limits. There was one day when we were sort of mobbed by a group of children. One of the kids leapt up and pulled my weapon, which made all of his friends laugh. Gently but firmly I tried to make it clear that they shouldn't try it again. Whatever I'd said obviously didn't work, since the next second another kid made a grab for the ammunition pouch on my webbing as I went to walk away.

'Whoah, whoah, cut it out.' The situation was beginning to get a bit uncomfortable. It was almost definitely innocent, and yet I wasn't interested in taking any chances. It could have been the lead-up to something ugly. People who let their guard down too often in Afghanistan didn't always come home. I tried to shoo them away back to their parents. As I turned around again to head off in the other direction, one of them lobbed a stone. It was more playful than vicious, but he'd crossed a line. At that point I realised that something more was needed. I fired a single round into a nearby puddle. That got the message across. The kids instantly scattered like a flock of pigeons and sped for the safety of a broken-down bit of wall a few metres away. We carried our patrol on in peace.

I might come across as overwhelmingly positive, but if you abuse that, you'll only get a certain number of warnings before I respond with extreme negativity. In seconds I can – and will – transform myself. Positivity isn't the same as weakness, and being nice doesn't mean that you'll let people walk over you. It's important to show others that you have boundaries and that you need them to be respected. Like with so much of life, things are far better if you keep them black and white. If you allow your personal relations to shift into the grey zone, it's likely they'll begin to deteriorate.

So if somebody is upsetting you, then you owe it to yourself – and to them – to let them know. No good ever came of bottling things up. You can't afford to let a small misunderstanding degenerate into a resentment just because you wanted to appear easy-going and pleasant.

Emilie

Anthony is definitely aware of his strengths and his weaknesses. He might not always show it, but he knows. He's so positive, his kids absolutely adore him, and he's got the biggest heart I've ever known. We never see the chief instructor in our home. That's not who Anthony is. He's a gentle guy, the sort of person who's kind to everyone. He wants the guy who opens the door at a club to feel as special as the guy managing it.

Getting on with people is one of his greatest skills. You can put him in a room with anyone and I guarantee that Anthony will be friends with them within minutes – it won't matter if it's a barrister or a binman – he'll find a way of connecting with them.

In the best possible sense he's like a chameleon. He knows how to act around everyone, what kind of body language to display, what sorts of things to say.

I think this is because he's unusually empathetic. You can see this in all of his interactions with others, even confrontations. Despite him being so positive (sometimes I think it's *because* he's so positive), we do occasionally end up having a blazing row. We're human, we both like to give as good as we get, and we both know how great it can feel to get things off your chest. But afterwards, when the smoke has cleared, he'll always want to talk it through. He'll say, 'We're going to sit down calmly now and resolve it.' And we always do come up with a solution.

We'll ask each other what it was that was annoying each of us and how we can stop something like that happening again. It's the brutal honesty Anthony never stops banging on about. Clear, 100 per cent honesty. That's what he believes in, and that's what he expects from other people. This desire to talk things through and really get to the bottom of the problem feels to me like something that comes naturally to women, but is a bit harder for a man. What drives it is his ability to always see the argument from my perspective, which is actually quite spooky sometimes. Especially because, when the red mist comes down, I'm not sure I'm able to look at things through his eyes.

Ultimately this means that whatever bad feeling there might have been between us never linger. He's not moody, he doesn't take his anger out on anybody else. By the time we've gone to bed, everything's back on an even keel.

LESSONS

When people confront you with negativity, don't be tempted to throw negativity back at them. Overwhelm them with positivity and you'll knock them off balance.

Sociability is a massively undervalued skill. Being able to get on with people is such a valuable tool to have in your locker, so work hard to make sure you're the sort of person other people want to be around. It will be worth it.

Cultivate your empathetic side. Being able to see things from another person's perspective is a massive advantage when you're trying to form a positive connection with them.

Sometimes the most positive thing you can do is say no. Saying no can be a positive affirmation of your instincts, the best way of furthering or preserving your interests. Other people might see it as a negative, but it's up to you to really determine its nature.

CHAPTER 4

KEEP IT SIMPLE

THERE'S NO FEELING like the aftermath of a successful mission. The Chinook would fly low on our journey home, and nine times out of ten I'd sit on the open tailgate beside the Minigun, my legs hanging over the edge. I must have looked like a kid without a care in the world. I'd look out and drink in the landscape. Its beauty could take your breath away, especially at that time in the morning when the sun rises, the dawn's light gradually illuminating the darkness of the valleys, catching the wisps of smoke drifting up from the buildings below as people began their days, blissfully unaware of what I'd just come through. Minutes before, I'd have been in a shit-hole warzone, but afterwards I'd just be thinking, 'Wow, look at this.' I used to see this feeling almost as a reward. For as long as I sat on that tailgate I'd give myself up to the emotions that I usually worked so hard to control. I'm still here, I'd say to myself. I've lived to see another day.

During these dawn rides I'd be dazed with triumph and the sheer elation of being alive. I used the time to reflect, as it was a good opportunity to unwind. Scenes from the past hours would pass through my mind – things I could have done better, things I'd got bang-on – and then they'd be gone, left in the valley forever. It was pretty black and white for me. If we'd achieved our objective and hadn't lost any men in the process, I didn't see much point in spending too much time dwelling on the night's events. The job was done, I had processed it and I'd never have to revisit it again. It was pure freedom to me.

You can do the same thing in your own life. Say, for example, you've come back from work having made a big fuck-up. The first thing you do is acknowledge the situation for what it is. Is it negative or positive? Get it into that black-and-white category. You've been bollocked by your boss? That's negative. What happened? Why did it happen? If it's a failure, fine. Everybody fails. We fail in the same way as we breathe air. It's just part of life. Self-loathing and self-recrimination won't help here. What *will* help is adopting a positive mindset, trying to work out where you went wrong so that you won't make the same mistake again.

It's not an automatic process; it requires effort on your part to dig down and find the positives. But what's exciting to me is that it's in your hands to shape how you respond to experiences, whether they're good or bad. There are always two different stories that can be told about any situation. It's up to you to make sure you tell the right one.

STAY OUT OF THE GREY ZONE

I'm always surprised by the reception I get when I do my tours. I'm not a scientist or a psychologist or anything like that; I'm just talking about my life, about what I've done. And usually, the things that I say speak to what people know already. I've got the mind of a simpleton. I've had so many people say to me, 'Ant, I knew that! I'm kicking myself because what you're saying is so obvious.'

The reason it's so obvious is that it's always been inside us. All of us. What hasn't always been there is the bullshit and the complication, the confusion that society is introducing. We spend so much time trying to figure the distractions out that there's no space for anything else. It's not a lightbulb moment. It's a kick-yourself moment. You have to strip the bullshit away. For me, things only make sense if I keep them black and white.

I've simplified my life to the two things I care most about: my family and my work. Nothing else matters. And it makes things so much more straightforward when you've identified what's most important to you and cut away all the bullshit. When I go to work, I'm in full work-mode and I give that job everything. When I get home, I'm a dad and a husband. As soon as I get home and close the door, that's it. Work doesn't exist anymore. No grey areas, no conflict.

Looking at life in black and white is also an important part of my positive mindset. I feel so much more confident and in control when I know exactly what I'm dealing with. What I try to avoid at all costs is slipping into the grey zone – that place where the edges of things go blurry. When you're faced with a decision or a scenario, just ask yourself: is it positive or negative? Right or wrong? Good or evil? If you don't know the answer, you'd be best off staying the fuck away.

This clarity means you can take ownership of everything you do, whatever the outcome. I love people who are like that, because they're decisive. There's no grey area, there's no time when they're sitting on the fence saying to themselves: 'Maybe it's this, maybe it's that.' Whether they get things right or wrong, they've kept it black and white. You can do the same.

STRIP IT ALL AWAY

Everybody should be doing this: conducting an audit of themselves and their priorities. Think about what matters most to you in life, and then ask yourself how you're actually spending your time. As far as I'm concerned, anything I do that diverts my attention and energy away from promoting the interests of either my career or my family is something I should look at cutting out because I know it will end up having a negative impact.

I try to make the same kind of assessment in all of my interactions with the world. What do I stand to gain from this? What could I lose? How does the prospect make me feel?

One thing that I know always triggers negativity in me is being forced to do something that doesn't sit right with me. Nine times out of ten I won't do it; to the point that if, say, I've agreed to do a bit of filming but then realise later on that I don't feel comfortable with it, I'll be willing to cover whatever production costs come up rather than go through with it. I know that people will accuse me of being a control freak, but it's not that: I control what I can control; if I can't control it, I stay away. It's so simple but so important.

DON'T GIVE YOURSELF OPTIONS

When you load yourself up with more questions to answer, more excuses, more escape routes, you might make your life a bit easier in the short term, but ultimately you'll get tangled up.

Part of what attracted me to *SAS: Who Dares Wins* was the sense that it represented a clean break, which meant that it was also a risk. Staying in the military, working in security – the routes most people in my position go down – obviously carried their own physical risks, but they were safe. I knew these worlds, I'd gone where I could in them and they'd become like a comfort blanket. They were that grey area.

When you have too many options in life, it becomes too easy. Like riding your bike with stabilisers on way longer than you need to. You find that you can always dig out an excuse to explain why you didn't persist with a project, or when doing something became a bit too challenging and you just dropped it in favour of doing something easier, even if you knew at the end of the day that the tricky task would end up being more profitable. It's harder when your options get reduced to a harsh choice between success and failure. But you'll surprise yourself. When you're forced to be courageous, when you find yourself standing up against that door, bullets smashing past you, you might think, 'Oh, here we go,' but you know you've got to get through it or otherwise you'll be stuck there, a sitting duck. Nine times out of ten you make it work for you.

I came away from the military with the mindset of, if I can do it at this extreme, brutally simplified level, what *can't* I achieve. I've carried that with me. I don't give myself ten options. I give myself two. And both of them are going to be extremely hard, but when I come out the other end they'll be way more rewarding. If it goes south, you can understand what exactly went wrong because everything has been in black and white. You'll have learned something. If it goes right, you'll know how to replicate that success.

Sometimes you'll find that those situations occur naturally. When you have a baby, your options narrow: unless you're a sociopath, you're not going to just walk away and let it die. Instead, you step up and work hard for the baby and your partner, because you have to. It can seem hairy at times, difficult to cope with, but it almost always works out.

At other times you'll need to take a leap. Say if you're considering starting a business outside your normal career. You could try to divide your time between your day job and your bit on the side, but you'll end up in the grey zone, where you're not properly committed to either activity, and both will suffer. Far better to throw yourself heart and soul into your new business. When you've stripped away your options there's always risk, but clarity and simplicity also have the potential to bring amazing rewards.

LIVE BY THE SWORD, DIE BY THE SWORD

The wall that separates military from civilian life is really high – far higher than most people might think. There are lots of small bricks in that wall, and two fucking big ones. If you're going into combat you have to be prepared for two possibilities: it's likely you might have to kill someone; and it's also likely that you might be killed or wounded.

Every day in the Marines I was faced with the possibility that by its end I might have killed another person, or been killed myself. Later on, in the Special Forces, where the regularity and danger of operations were ramped up massively, this feeling would be exaggerated a million times over. I coped with this by reducing the two ideas to their most elemental levels.

A large part of my job in the SBS was hunting, and then killing, human beings. I could have complicated this and gone into every operation thinking to myself: this is just another person, maybe a husband, maybe a father. He's not so different to me. But in doing that I knew I'd be slipping into the grey zone.

Instead, I reminded myself that most of the people we were going after were bad fuckers; we had hard evidence that they were responsible for head-spinningly cruel atrocities. There was one guy whose MO was strapping eight-year-olds with suicide vests to wheelbarrows filled with explosives and covered with hay, and forcing them to push them near a British patrol. Once close enough, this villain, sitting at a safe distance, would set the kid's vest off. I had no problem going after someone like that. As far as I was concerned, that level of evil just didn't deserve to be walking on this planet. If I wasn't going to do it, somebody else would. You're on the list, mate.

And even when I was so close to the enemy that I shot people in the face, I made sure never to look them in the eye. I knew my weapon was in the right place, so I tried to look through them. I had no need to make it a personal encounter. They weren't people, they were targets. *Boom boom.* He's dropped. On to the next target. I kept it simple, reducing everything to its bare essentials.

As confident as I always was that I wouldn't get hit, I wasn't delusional. I knew that there was a chance that I might get careless, or one of the Taliban might get lucky and I'd be killed or grievously wounded. I had to find a way to cope with the insane levels of risk that I, or comrades I cared about, was exposed to. I did this by stripping what I did down to its simplest elements.

My attitude was: if you live by the sword, you should expect to die by the sword. If you're a big-scale Class A drug dealer, you should probably be prepared to do twenty years in prison. You're out there, so you have to be willing to suffer the consequences. When you're an elite operator landing on targets guarded by the Taliban, you can't afford to be *surprised* when they start firing back. What do you expect?

That was always my mindset. When I cut everything else away, I knew I was willing to live with the repercussions of my actions. I went through the same process when considering how I felt about the prospect of others being killed. Again, I started with acknowledging the black-and-white facts of the situation. When you go on tour, you know that not everyone in your unit is going to come back. Was I sad when we lost guys? Absolutely. There was never a death that did not feel like a tragedy to me. But did I accept there was a risk of that before I took the job? Yes, 100 per cent.

All we could do was give our pal the best send-off we possibly could, celebrate his life, then move on to the next job. It sounds harsh, but to my mind it was the only way I could process a situation of such magnitude. It wasn't about turning off my emotions, it was about creating a framework within which I could understand them and make them work for me. Because I knew before we even departed home soil that there was a strong possibility that one of us might get killed, I'd already accepted 50 per cent of that emotional burden – the hard work was already done.

I have almost no memory of those times I held bleeding comrades in my arms. That's my coping mechanism, my positive, simplifying mindset stepping in to protect me. The details are doubtless still there in some recess of my mind, and I could probably reconstruct every painful moment of those dark events if I had to. But I don't. It wouldn't be right, for one thing. More than that, there's no need. No good can come of digging those experiences up and complicating things; it won't enhance who I am.

Everybody in my fire team would have found a different way of rationalising the situation; this was mine. It was an example of why it's so important to exercise and expose your emotions. If I hadn't done that before I joined the Special Forces, I know for a fact that I'd have ended up in a shit state, broken by the pain of seeing men I cared for die. And if I'd allowed that to happen, then it's easy to see how PTSD could have swallowed up my career, my marriage, my ability to function in the world. There's nothing to be gained from pretending that you won't be affected by grief or fear; they're life events that everybody will be exposed to. It's a paradox – the more you pretend to yourself and others that you're unaffected by these things, the more vulnerable you'll leave yourself to them when they strike. And they will. Grief and fear are as inevitable as death and taxes. That was as true for me as an elite operator in the Special Forces as it is for someone living a quiet life working in a call centre. The only difference is that my career meant that those turbulent, frightening emotions were ever-present. They had to be confronted there and then.

DECISIONS ARE ONLY AS HARD AS YOU LET THEM BE

This emotionally connected, black-and-white framework is even more valuable when you're actually in combat. In the SBS we conducted our missions in an ultra-methodical style. At all times we tried to be calm – moving smoothly, method-ically from one room of a compound to the next. If I were to burst through a door screaming at the top of my voice and found a group of women and children in front of me, the chances are they'd be panicked by the way I'd just exploded into view. They'd erupt suddenly and run in every direction, compromising my safety and the mission's success. The last thing we wanted was for the situation to degenerate into a chaotic free-for-all. It would have been far more dangerous and would have made our jobs significantly harder. Obviously, this wasn't always possible, and sometimes things got very noisy very quickly, but mostly this was exactly what we were able to achieve. One of the key factors in this was that we reduced our decision-making to the simplest possible terms.

Every decision we took was easy because we made it easy. People say to me, 'Oh, it must have been so hard to weigh everything up.' It's only as hard as you let it be. We were given our orders, and anything that came between us and our mission objective was a problem that needed to be solved. It was black and white.

Say we were on a mission to capture an IED facilitator. There'd be a briefing beforehand where we'd be told that the target was responsible for the deaths of X number of British Marines. We were after a bad guy. Simple. It was obvious he needed to be brought in. We get to the target location and we're met with fierce resistance. It's kill or be killed. Again, it's simple. If you want to stay alive, you kill. If you're faced with a Taliban firing at you, you shoot back.

We've kicked the door down into one of the buildings and found women and children in the first room we enter. Do we need to do anything to them? No. Or what if we burst into a room where moments ago the guy we find there has been unloading bullets through the door, but has now shit himself and dropped his weapon? I could put a couple of rounds into him, but is he a threat anymore? No. We can detain him without any trouble and pass him on to the next team. It's done. Simple.

It's not rocket science. If I'd tried to complicate that situation in any way, I guarantee I wouldn't be sitting here writing this now. And, as well as it served me in combat, this approach is something that works just as well in normal life. You have to learn to resist that temptation to overcomplicate things. If you're tasked with coming up with a plan at work, try to frame every choice you make in the simplest possible terms. If you can't explain to others what you want them to do in a sentence, the plan is too complicated and they'll struggle to execute it. Plus, the more you load that plan up with complicating elements, the more likely you are to end up being paralysed by doubt and indecision.

DON'T BE A BULLY WITH A WEAPON

When you're a front-line soldier you're the arbiter of life and death. There's a massive responsibility that comes with that knowledge. You're making big decisions the whole time and you don't get second chances. It's up to you to decide who's a threat and who's not. It's up to you to take that extra glance to see if there are women and children in that vehicle; to assess whether that Taliban is about to drop his weapon or fire at you. That's the difference between a good soldier and an elite soldier. It's a big responsibility. You have to make those decisions and, at the end of the day, you've got to live with them.

I know too many guys who are haunted by the things they've done or seen. Calls they've made – whether they're right or wrong – are still reverberating in their brains, years after they last picked up a gun.

I want to live my life with no regrets, and so I make sure that every time I make a decision I do it for a positive reason. Now, if I'm involved in something at work, I'll always take time to ask myself: am I approaching it in this particular way because it's the best means of ensuring the best outcome, or am I just doing it because it's a shortcut? I know from experience that if I opt for the easier route, that decision will come back to bite me. It's such a negative way of thinking, and it only ends up creating more trouble further down the line.

This pull between positive and negative was something I saw all the time when I was in the military. The first thing you want to do when you go on operations is fire your weapon. Every soldier wants to get a kill. I don't mean in a reckless, vicious way. But you do have this deep urge to get into a firefight. What else are you there for? Everything you've trained for is leading up to that moment when you pull the trigger for the first time.

What you must become careful about is not becoming that dog with a bloodlust. Once a dog bites, it'll bite again and again. It can be the same with some men. They taste that blood and find it hard, very hard, not to shoot again for the sake of it. Suddenly, you know you're capable of breaking one of mankind's great taboos. The thing you *thought* you could do, you now know you *can* do. There's no going back. After that, firing with blanks feels like playing at being soldiers. What's the fucking point? You want the responsibility of having a live weapon with live rounds. You don't want a toy.

The power – the positivity – comes from knowing that you could pull the trigger, probably without any consequences at all, but you don't. Anyone can point and pull. It takes something more to coolly assess whether the man standing across from you with a wild, scared look in his eyes and an AK-47 hanging limply by his side – a weapon that only moments before he'd been firing at you – is an imminent threat. You could justify it. Just brush it under the carpet. But ask yourself, is it the right thing to do? Do you want to go to the grave haunted by his pleading face?

There's one scene that still sometimes flashes into my mind. We were searching for a high-value target. We'd dealt with the men in the courtyard who'd been firing at us aggressively. There was no question at that point that it was right to shoot back. Then one of them picked his weapon up and ran through a doorway in front of me. I was behind a wall, focusing on the doorway, certain that he would be our next target.

He moved, poking his head out through the doorway, a bit like a meerkat popping up out of his hole. From my position I could see that he had his weapon down while he couldn't see me. I positioned my sights to sit right onto his head. *Here we go*, I thought to myself. On its heels came another thought. *His weapon's down, he's shitting himself. I could fire now, make my life easy, but it wouldn't be cool.* I was making more work for myself. If I didn't take him down we'd have to go into that room, disarm him. To this day I don't think he realises how close he came to being rubbed out. If I'd been a dog rather than a soldier, he'd have got it. One million per cent.

Being in control confers more power. I made the positive decision. I was in the zone, making decisions in split seconds. Only moments before I'd been ready to take out anything with a gun that moved; this then gave way to a period of what felt like hours in which my sights hovered on his head. When you keep things simple, you'll find it far easier to identify those times when just because you *can* do something, it doesn't mean you *should* do it.

I've found that, overwhelmingly, when you make a decision for the right reasons, it will work out far better. But when it does go wrong, if you know in your heart of hearts that you were sincere in what you wanted to achieve, it makes failure far easier to cope with. You're not assailed by self-recrimination. You don't have that little voice inside your head nagging away: 'You know why this happened, don't you? It's because you couldn't be bothered to do it properly.' Instead, you can dust yourself off, pluck out the lessons you've learned from the situation, and move on.

Emilie

I was delighted for Anthony when he joined the Marines. It was blindingly obvious that he needed a path in life and going back into the military opened a new one out. He knew that this was what he wanted to do.

It opened up new paths for me to follow too. At the time I worked for Cancer Research in London, commuting in from Chelmsford. As soon as Ant went back into the military I realised that this wasn't going to work for me anymore, so I retrained as a beauty therapist. I did that up until our daughter Priseïs was born. She was our third child, and that felt as good a time as any to become a housewife.

I'd made my peace with the idea that my husband would be fighting a war on the other side of the world, and that this would change everything for the family that he'd left back home on the base. Our contact with him was limited to one conversation a week. I'd make sure I was home every Sunday afternoon, so when he called I'd be there. I'd have hated it if he'd rung and I didn't answer.

Otherwise, my philosophy was: if I'm sitting here worrying about him, then I'm not getting on with my life.

I never watched the news when Anthony was in Afghanistan. I never used to sit there thinking, 'Is he in danger? Is he in a firefight?' I didn't allow myself to do this, because I knew it would pull me apart. I told myself, if he were to die on the battlefield it would be horrendous for us, but he'd have been killed doing what he loved. Nobody forced him to put a uniform on and go out there. It might sound brutal to you. Fine. You cope in the way you can.

I had to carry on being me. I didn't want the children to grow up in a household that felt brittle and afraid and full of anxiety. I didn't want them surrounded by negative energy.

But his absolute confidence that he wouldn't get hit, even during those really savage days in the war when people around him were getting injured, helped me. Hand on heart, I never ever worried about him coming back. I always knew that at the end of the tour he'd be strolling through our front door. This wasn't me sticking my head in the sand and pretending that accidents couldn't happen in combat. It was more that I knew that there was no point worrying about something that hadn't happened yet. You can't let the unknown control your life.

Once he was back we'd talk about what he'd been doing. It would have been weird if six months of his life remained a kind of black hole to me. But I avoided dwelling on what he told me. It was almost like it would go in one ear and come out the other straight away. He'd tell me something and I wouldn't retain it. Again, it was my way of dealing with the situation.

When he joined the Special Forces, everything became even more intense. This was true even when he was stationed at home. Some nights, Anthony would get a call during dinner and just disappear. One moment we'd be eating pasta together, the next I'd be putting it in a sandwich box for him to eat down the line. He'd come back from the briefing and say, 'We're going now. I can't say where I'm going, and I can't say when I'll be back.' And that was that. Occasionally, if I did put the news on later that evening I could piece together where he might be. But more often I'd be in the dark.

What was really important to us was that the violence and trauma from his work in the Special Forces never spilled over into the safe, happy home we'd built together. I remember one time him coming home from six months in Afghanistan. We never talked in too much detail on the phone, but we had code words we could use to communicate things, and of course the other wives talked among themselves. I knew it had been really nasty. Shyla had a Barbie tent back then. The second Anthony walked in he dived straight into the tent. He started playing with the dolls, talking to them as Shyla clambered all over him. I remember being amazed, thinking, 'You've gone from all the brutality, to *this*. That's a lot for me to take in. How are *you* processing it?'

For him it was simple. He had a work head, and a home head. The second he came into the family home, the work head came off. The second he left it again, that was it. We weren't in his thoughts anymore. Everything was black and white.

It was something I loved about him. This very old-school manliness, which meant he could go out onto the battlefield, and then, when he came home, he wouldn't bring any of that with him. The warrior had disappeared. In his place was a sweet, caring father.

LESSONS

Stay out of the grey zone. If you keep things black and white, your life will be so much more straightforward, and everything that happens to you will be easier to process.

Not all questions need to be answered. In fact, not all questions need to be posed. Don't get lost in overthinking situations. Learn what you need from them and move on.

Actions have consequences. If you aren't willing to take responsibility for what you're about to do or say, maybe it's time to think again.

Strip your life down to the essentials and try to work out what's most important to you. It could be your family, or your career, or a particular passion. If there's anything obstructing or complicating your priorities, you should consider cutting it away.

Decisions are only as hard as you make them. Focus on what's essential. Don't get sidetracked by distractions.

CHAPTER 5

CHANGE OR DIE

SOME PEOPLE ARE born warriors. They have an affinity with violence and everything that comes with it. They like fighting other human beings. It's all they want to do from an early age. That was never me. I didn't grow up dreaming of being a soldier, I just happened to be extremely good at it.

The military was never my first choice of career. Come to think of it, it wasn't even my second. I'd started out thinking I might be a footballer. And for a while it looked as if that might actually happen. When I was a teenager I went to live in a football academy in France and even came back to England to have trials at Southampton. The trials never really came to anything, and as time passed I felt my enthusiasm for football wane. I liked it, but I didn't like it enough.

After that I thought about becoming a photographer. It seemed like an exciting, creative trade that would enable me to travel the world. And yet I realised that I had neither the time nor the resources needed to really make it. I had no contacts who could help me get a foot in the door, and no real sense of how or even where I should start out. How would I keep myself alive while I built a career? I just didn't know. By contrast, I knew that in the military I'd be fed and watered and get a wage every month. It was the perfect balance of being looked after while offering me an escape from the life I was leading. A small village in rural France is a great place to grow up and a great place to grow old. But if you're an ambitious young lad, it feels like a dead end. It was a straightforward choice: do I throw myself into a career loaded down with complications, or do I keep it simple?

As I went on I found that being in the military was an eye-opening experience. I went to parts of the world I'd have never imagined going to, I learned amazing skills, I experienced things that very few people will ever get to see. All of this made me a better, more rounded human being.

Eventually I joined the Special Forces because I wanted to put myself into the most exciting, demanding place I could. For a long time it was exactly that, and I couldn't imagine ever wanting to do anything else. But when you've done three tours of Afghanistan, when you've kicked countless doors down and done hundreds of Tier One operations, that changes. It got to the point where, for me, the missions on which I *didn't* pull the trigger were a success. It was so different to the early days, when I actively wanted to be getting into firefights. As soon as I realised that, I knew it was time to go. I needed a new challenge.

When I left the Special Forces, I reckoned that there would be an easy transition into civilian life. I had a head start, or so I thought, because I'd been a part of an elite organisation. Surely it wouldn't take me long to find my feet. I'd shown the resilience, focus and grit to get to the top inside the military, so I was confident I could replicate that in the world outside.

It turns out I was wrong, although I wouldn't find out quite how wrong I'd been for a good few months. The problem was that despite knowing I was ready for something else, I just didn't know what that something else was. Not yet.

When it comes down to it, you can do one of two things when you leave the military: go into security or become a PT. Sixteen years of elite training, of savage fights in warzones, and you end up working the door of a nightclub or helping housewives lose weight. Neither really appealed to me, but I had bills to pay and a family to raise, so, while I worked out what to do, I jumped straight into a security job: escorting a superyacht from the Maldives to the south of France. I started the very next day after I left uniform. One job led to another, and a few months later I was still doing the same thing.

To begin with it was cool and exciting. We went to beautiful places and it was good being flown about on someone else's pound. There was reassurance in knowing that although officially the safety net that the military had once provided had disappeared, there was still an informal network of ex-Special Forces guys who arranged jobs for you. I knew lots of former operators who planned to do that for the rest of their working life. It's good money. It's usually pretty easy. Why not?

But I had this voice in my head saying, 'Are you going to be doing this until you die?' I didn't want to be working for a pay cheque until it was time to retire. I knew myself, and knew that I liked things to be done my way. I'm a leader with a different way of thinking and working. It's been like that through my whole career. It's always been, 'Oh, where's Ant?' 'He's off doing his own thing again.' I like grabbing things and then improving them. There was no scope for either of those things doing security jobs.

And I was bored. So fucking bored. I missed the sense of purpose I'd had in the military, where I knew I was doing something meaningful and worthwhile. By contrast, working in private security is *dull*. People have watched too much TV, so they have this big image of what it means to be a bodyguard. I'll tell you this: you're not out there saving Whitney Houston's life and then falling in love with each other. You're a glorified babysitter. I was looking after people like Kate Beckinsale, the band Evanescence, fending off the occasional rogue autograph-hunter or overenthusiastic photographer. Compared with everything I'd done before, it was beyond mundane.

Looking back now, I realise that I'd wanted to throw myself into a job so I could put off confronting the strangeness of life outside the military. There's no psychological preparation for civvy street. There's practical stuff, like offering you the chance to go on a physical training instructors' course, or a security managers' course, or whatever. It's all well and good, but those courses mean jack shit if you're not mentally ready for what's about to come.

The thing that shocked me was that in my head, all I was doing was leaving one organisation to join another; in reality, they're two different worlds. In the military, once you've passed training and joined your unit you have to act like a soldier. If you don't, you won't last long. It's the same on the other side. The fact of having left the military isn't enough to make you a civilian; you have to learn how to behave like one too. The problem is that there's lots of intense, highly professional training to help you learn how to be a soldier. There isn't anything for those men going to the other way.

Your mind needs to be systematically retrained. In the military, everything is designed to prepare you for war. Specifically, the government spent over a million pounds training me to meet violence with extreme violence. You're taught to counter aggression with extreme aggression. This is drilled into you over and over again, and reinforced when you actually get into combat. It becomes second nature. This is all well and good when you're in a firefight in Afghanistan – it's the thing that will probably save your life – but a disaster on the streets of Chelmsford.

This element was even more present in those of us who fought in the Special Forces. During my two tours to

Afghanistan we were out on operations night after night after night, for six months at a time. We weren't like the old guys who'd served in the Special Forces in the 1980s and 1990s, who had to squabble over who got to go on the one mission that came up that year, then talked about it endlessly for the next few decades. For us, that life had become our normality.

Everything was flipped. My life was kicking doors down, whacking people, saving people. My life was the pistol attached to my leg, the knife and grenades attached to my chest. These were my clothes. If they weren't strapped to me, I felt naked. I slept with my weapons beneath my bed, and this was as ordinary to me as the slippers or phone charger most normal people keep there. It would have been stranger for me to go to Tesco's than it would to storm a compound in a remote village in Afghanistan. Where other people pondered what coffee to order at the till of Costa, I was there in our storeroom, trying to decide whether the next mission looked hairy enough to justify taking a light anti-tank weapon.

The problem is that you can't become that person and then just take it all off when you feel like it, as if it's a pair of old boots. It's not a trick you're playing or an act you're putting on. It *is* you. You control it most of the time, of course, but it's always there.

In the world outside the military there is, quite rightly, zero tolerance towards violence and aggression. What saved your skin in a warzone will land you in prison in civilian life, or at the very least have you categorised as somebody with grievous anger-management issues. It's fucking dangerous and is barely acknowledged. There are thousands of men walking around with that element inside them, ready to explode at any moment. I should know. For a long time I was one of them.

There was another layer related to this that was more personal to me. Life in the military had not just instilled a lethal level of aggression in me, it had fundamentally changed who I was. From about seventeen, eighteen onwards, after I got absorbed into life in the military, I'd changed quickly. The laid-back French culture I'd acquired as a kid was discarded because I realised that being in uniform was all about the survival of the fittest. I'd left the Paras because I knew that it was a toxic environment to be in, but although the attitude was different in lots of ways in the Marines and Special Forces, neither was a space where you could afford to show any weakness or vulnerability. They were still brutal, boozy, British places, so the immaculate, naïve, skinny seventeen-year-old with blue eyes and thick black eyebrows that met in the middle disappeared.

Instead, I developed a suit of armour that I kept on until I left the Special Forces when I was thirty-two. That suit of armour protected the emotional, energetic, sensitive lad I'd been before I picked up a rifle. It kept me from being picked on and bullied, and was exactly the sort of persona that thrived in the world I had entered. There's no way I could have achieved what I did without it. I think, however, that somewhere along the way I forgot that I could take it off. When I handed my uniform in, I kept my suit of armour on. In doing so, I was storing up trouble for myself.

As the months went by, I was still really struggling to do the basics of running my life. The military had taken care of everything for us. When you get married, they provide married quarters. They sorted out your taxes and your bills. All you have to do is turn up and wipe your arse. And then, suddenly, when you leave, you've got to deal with stuff like council tax, rent payments, electricity bills. So at the same time as I was trying to figure out how the new world I'd entered worked, and how I fitted into it, all these small stresses were being forced upon me. It felt like death by a thousand cuts. At the back of my mind was the knowledge that those ex-soldiers who didn't adapt ended up in prison for a long stretch, or drinking heavily, or addicted to drugs, or a down and out. I'd seen it happen so many times to so many of the other guys I'd seen leave the military before me. For a while it looked like it would happen to me too.

When you're as bored and frustrated as I was, you try to fill the time. I felt disengaged by my work life, so I concentrated on my social life. I was drinking far more than I'd done in the military. Back then, a bad hangover might have slowed my responses enough to have been fatal, so I was careful about how much I put away. Now the worst it meant was a rough morning. The old boundaries had been lifted and I was enjoying the fresh air of freedom. And why not? I felt like I'd earned it.

I started to behave like the men in the Paras I'd been so keen to distance myself from all those years ago. I was more 'Airborne' when I was out of the regiment than I'd ever been when I was inside it. It was as if I'd woken up and just decided to be a complete dickhead. I couldn't even begin to explain why. For a good few months I was the life and soul of every party. I was wild back then, and I can see how the extremely full-on, out-there energy I possessed at the time could have come across as too much for some. Let's put it this way: if you were an introvert, I probably would have been your worst nightmare. I can see now how I could have come across as intimidating, even threatening. Although people always knew I wasn't a bully, they'd either want to be bound tight into my group or run a thousand miles. There was no in between. I was out to have fun; anything else that happened was secondary.

I think it was a delayed adolescence – some part of me wanting to experience the things I'd denied myself in the past. I'd had a kid early, married early, and now there were no rules, or at least that's how it seemed at the time. Looking back, I wonder whether there's something about military life that prevents men from growing up in the normal way. You have to be so adult about so much, and yet parts of your personality remain undeveloped.

Whenever I went out, Emilie would expect to get a call from one of my mates, or the police, to say that I'd got into another fight. I never actually liked fighting. I've seen enough of it as its most vicious, savage extreme, so I know what proper combat does. For a while, though, it just happened. I'd get started on by men who saw me as another alpha male to be taken down, or had heard I'd been in the Special Forces and wanted to make a name for themselves, or who just thought I was looking at their girlfriend. Someone would push me too far and I'd go from polite and respectful to, 'Fucking how dare you. You're going to fucking get it.' There was no in-between stage. If you crossed that line, I'd annihilate you.

Too many mornings I woke up with a sickening hangover and a bleary sense that I'd done something bad the night before. It was so hard for Emilie to see me during that phase. As soon as I walked out the door she'd be on edge. I don't know if she ever slept.

That behaviour also stopped me from being the father I should have been. You can't be a good dad if you wake up drunk and desperate for sleep or, worse, in a police cell. I could see how Emilie's anxiety about me was spreading to the children – kids pick up on so much. I cringe now when I think of all those days I could have spent with them that were wasted, or lost. When I look back I think, 'I put her through *that*, and she stayed with me; she must have loved me.'

And still I carried on. There were no positive voices in my life urging me to stop. Perhaps if my father hadn't passed away when I was so young, he could have been the man to step in. I didn't stop going out, because I told myself that it was never me who instigated the fights. I wasn't picking on people or searching violence out. It came to me. I was making mistake after mistake after mistake, and I failed to heed the warning signs. It could only end in jail. And thank fuck it did. I was sentenced to fourteen months in prison. I served five months, with a further two on tag, and seven on probation.

I had a lot of time during which to reflect behind bars. I realised how much I needed what had taken place. I sometimes think that they were the best five months of my life; the best thing that had ever happened to me. Imagine if I'd got off. How invincible would I have felt if I'd beaten up a police officer and got away with it? What would my next violent offence have been? I'd have been looking at ten years. It happened at exactly the right time in my life. Any later, and I don't know if I'd have been able to escape the existence I'd fallen into. In the end, I was fortunate. I didn't get killed or disfigured. When I did go to prison it was only for a short term. And, most significantly of all, I didn't lose my wife, who is the ultimate foundation of everything that I do.

I looked around and felt truly humbled – I saw that I was no different to anybody else in there. I was the same as the smackhead, the same as the guy who was there for robbing houses. I was a scumbag like them, just a number. However we'd got there, we'd all ended up behind the same door.

I remember thinking to myself, 'Look where you are. Look how your family is suffering.' I was used to working away from home, so in that respect being in prison was no hardship. But I was also used to providing for my family, and I couldn't do that from a prison cell. I'd become a burden.

I had another even more significant light-bulb moment. After a couple of months, I realised that nobody from the military had come to visit me. I'd been telling myself that we were a band of brothers, with a bond like no other. Then I went to prison, and the only people that were there for me were my wife, my brother, my uncle and one friend. Nobody from the Marines or Special Forces wanted anything to do with me anymore.

The moment you leave the armed forces, you're on your own. My problem was that I hadn't understood that fact until I was sent to prison. Discovering it for myself was a liberation. Prison made me realise that if I was ever going to turn my life around, I'd have to take total ownership of it. Everything else was stripped away and I was faced with a stark choice: I could either wallow in my misery and perish, or start to build. I had to do this by myself. I couldn't rely on my military mindset or my military friends. The positive was that I knew that everything I created from that moment on would be mine alone. I owed nothing to nobody, and nobody owed anything to me.

I felt so free coming out of prison because I'd hit rock bottom. I was scraping away at the brick, trying to find foundations amid the rubble. I had to initiate a spell of brutal honesty with myself. Why do I keep ending up in fights? Why do I keep making the same mistake again and again and a-fucking-gain? Why had I been in prison? You have to think about your mistakes, because nobody else will. Do the hard yards. It's 100 per cent on you to work out that problem. But when you do, you'll know what you need to do to change. The harder you fall, the harder you'll have to work to flip yourself back up. But you know what? The rewards you'll get will be out of proportion to anything you could have ever imagined.

It was only then that I saw how much new space the changes I'd been going through had opened up. For years, the people I'd loved the most in the world had come second to the military's demands. Whenever I was asked to go somewhere at the drop of a hat, I went; whatever I was asked to do, I did. No matter how much my wife and children needed me, they had to accept that the Special Forces came first. The difference is, of course, that to Emilie and the children I'm a husband and a father and a friend, someone with a beating heart. As far as the military was concerned, I was an expensively trained asset. No more, no less. I'd been so immersed in that world that until I took that step out of it, I hadn't seen how unbalanced my priorities had been.

I was also forced to think about the suit of armour I'd put on. The moment I walked out of the prison gates I buckled down. For sure, I still had a few ups and downs, but in time I was able to shed that body armour, which, far from protecting me as it once had, was actually leading me into trouble. As soon as I realised the suit's potential for negativity, I hung the sword and the helmet and the breastplate up. The shame I felt helped me strip off the layers of armour I'd acquired over the past two decades. Slowly I returned to being the emotionally connected boy I'd once been; it turns out that you always revert back to who you *really* are. The only difference was that now I had all this life experience, awareness and clarity I could draw upon. I felt a physical sense of relief. Lighter, freer and, this was the real surprise, more like a man. All that time I thought I was being a man, I'd actually been behaving like a kid.

BE THE CHAMELEON

Change is the one constant in life. It's often something that's out of your control, and can be unsettling, even alarming. Approaching it with a positive mindset will enable you to cope when it turns your existence upside down and help you learn to embrace it as a dynamic, life-enhancing tool.

People who treat change as a positive force are able to adapt to any situation, because the human mind is incredible. When you're a kid you can absorb so much. You can drop a child into any situation, and they've almost always got the adaptability to be able to work things out and thrive – just as I had in northern France after the death of my father. And yet many of us lose that ability as we grow up. We think we're incapable of change, that in some sense we're the finished product. But this is so wrong. We should be aiming to evolve and improve and change until the day we stop breathing.

Change opens up new spaces for us and gives us the chance to learn new skills. Most of all, it challenges us. It can be arduous – at times you can feel as if it's knocked you off your feet – but if you embrace change, if you cultivate a chameleon-like adaptability, it will serve you well in life.

Look at the different careers I've had. Because I've learned to embrace change as a positive quality, I feel as if I can fit in everywhere. It makes such a difference if instead of fearing new situations – approaching them with a negative mindset – you dive straight into them. Now I relish the idea of being plonked in a situation where I haven't got a clue what's going on, and have to figure it out there and then. The process of adapting is fascinating. I might not know where I'll end up, but I'm pretty sure it's going to be interesting. Most of all, though, I know it's another chance to become a better version of myself.

CHANGE IS A LIFELONG PROJECT

The process of breaking yourself down and building yourself up again should be exactly that, a process. Something that goes on and on, with you adding a new layer each time. You should never feel that you've come to the end of your journey.

Not everyone seems to realise that. There's what I call the Zuckerberg effect: the idea that so many have that if they can just do one thing – develop one app, open just one door – it will change everything about their lives. Maybe a tiny fraction of people are going to do that. The rest of us have to go about it in a different way. A career is more than just one change; what you have to understand is that eventually all these little changes will add up.

If you reckon that your toolbox is full, then what have you got to look forward to? Why restrict your possibilities to enhance the way you think, to evolve? I cannot wait to find out what I'm going to be thinking, *how* I'm going to be thinking, when I'm eighty. I cannot wait. I'm going to be on this journey until the day I die – that's what gives my life purpose. I know I'm never going to reach the answer of who I really am and what I'm capable of. But, fuck me, I'm going to get as close as I possibly can.

You should never see yourself as the finished article. People have contacted me to tell me that they're sixty, or seventy, and thought that it was too late to change their mindset, but that my books and programmes taught them that they couldn't have been further from the truth. Your body will get to a stage where you'll realise that you can't do the things you used to be able to do when you were younger. But if you commit to change as a lifelong project, then your mind can get stronger and stronger and stronger, and one day you'll be sitting there, and it's possible your mind will be all that you have left. You can't ever let yourself get to the stage where you're afraid of being left alone with your brain because you've never spent time learning how to control it.

CUT OLD TIES

It took me a long time – far too long – to accept that I'd left the military. For ages, I used my experiences there as a crutch, succumbing to the temptation to cling to an organisation I felt comfortable in. I was making up excuses to go back on camp, and the fact that I was working security jobs for companies run by ex-SBS guys meant that I kept a foot in that old world.

This was understandable. In leaving, I'd not just lost the quarters that had been provided to me, I'd also lost the identity and sense of belonging that had been so much a part of my existence for so long. If you've been in the Special Forces, you're used to that sense of pride that comes from knowing that you're in an elite unit. You spend years telling your comrades how brilliant you all are; soldiers from the regular army treat you with deference. But in civvy street, very few people give a flying fuck. You're starting out again at the bottom of the pile. The guy in the council office you're talking to about sorting your tax out couldn't care less about the time you spent kicking down doors.

I knew I had to accelerate that transition from soldier to civilian. And if I wanted to do that, then I'd have to cut those old ties that were holding me back. Sometimes the things that feel safe and reassuring are actually the things that are slowly starving us of the oxygen we need to grow to our potential. Change offers you a natural opportunity to move on from tired old habits, ways of thinking and connections. Positivity is what gives you the courage you need to make this leap.

The idea of joining the 'Once a Marine, always a Marine' crowd was like a living death to me. I didn't want to be one of those sad fuckers who hang about with their military mates, telling shit stories down the boozer every weekend. I remember when I was younger, I'd go to pubs and the people I was with would point out old guys at the bar. 'There's Jimmy, he used to be in the Marines.' My reaction then was, 'Cool.' Now, I'm much more likely to think, 'Poor Jimmy, he's seventy, got diddly-squat, sitting at the end of the bar, telling the same shit story over and over again, making his Guinness last six hours. Ah, my fucking life.'

When I look back, I can tell myself that one of the best things I've done is to break free of that military circle and made a success of civilian life. And I fight hard to avoid being sucked back in. The fact that the Special Forces told me that I couldn't talk about anything from the moment I joined to the moment I left was almost a blessing. I'll never forget the time I spent in the military. There's so much I'm grateful for, so much I admire, but to get to where I am, I had to take the person that I'd been trained to be, then break it all the way down.

I knew there were lots of positives I wanted to keep hold of: communication, teamwork, leadership, planning, discipline. I then systematically got rid of everything else. Can you imagine what it would be like to have Ant Middleton, the chief instructor from *SAS: Who Dares Wins*, in your life 24/7? Nobody wants that. People get bored of that very, very, very quickly. That's the persona I put back on the shelf.

There's nothing worse for me now than going to a military reunion. I find myself getting quite anxious and angry and snappy because I feel as if I'm being dragged back into being the old Ant. I get people I don't know coming up to me and saying, 'Ant, fucking hell, you was a fucking cabbage hat,' referring to the green berets we used to wear, and all I really want to say is, 'Fuck off with your military banter. I don't know you. If you still want to be like that, go back into the military. Don't trouble us with that nonsense anymore.'

I've deliberately cut out military slang from my vocabulary. Or at least as much as I can, although the odd 'affirmative' sometimes pops out if someone asks me if I've done something. When I catch myself using it in text messages or whatever, I'll delete it immediately. Again, it's not because I think I'm too good for the military or anything; I'm just not in the services anymore, so why should I carry on acting as if I am? When I was a Marine I spoke like a Marine. Now I'm a civilian, I'll speak like a civilian.

I think differently now. I make business opportunities for myself. I don't think I'd be able to do that if was still tapping out text messages that said, 'That's hoofin', royal.' I worry about falling back into all that mindset, because I know that in some ways it would be the easy option.

I'm not deluded. I know that even if I were to become a tech guru making billions of pounds, I'll always be known as that Special Forces guy – and I don't want to deny that part of my history. And yet I do want to get to the point where the military represents only a small part of my life. That's not arrogance, or because I don't appreciate everything they did for me, and the amazing things men in uniform are doing on a daily basis. It's about me wanting to grow as an individual.

I'll bump into guys I used to know, and they'll say, 'Oh, you've changed.' I'll reply, 'I haven't seen you for eight years. I fucking *hope* I've changed.' To say that to me is the biggest compliment you can pay. I'd hope that if you saw me in another eight years you'd say the same thing. I don't want to be a one-dimensional person.

EMBRACE NEW PERSPECTIVES

Just because something used to work for you doesn't mean it will work for ever. In the first months after I left the Special Forces, I found I was deploying a very military mindset to try to solve very civilian problems. It was all smoke up the middle and attack the enemy, crash crash crash, let's get this sorted. This just doesn't work with people who don't wear a uniform. I soon found that this attitude, which was what I knew best, alienates other people.

The military way of thinking is in a sense very narrow and conformist. If you get a bunch of Paras together, you won't find much thinking outside the box. It's not like civilian life, where people come to a job and everyone has genuinely different perspectives. Even for me, coming from the Special Forces where we were encouraged to think much more for ourselves, it was quite overwhelming to discover how varied people's opinions were. At times it could be a bit like there were a thousand different radios playing a thousand different songs at the same time. I couldn't grasp it, and ended up feeling like a kid who's been told he's done something wrong but doesn't understand why.

If I came up with a suggestion, and then somebody disagreed and put forward an idea of their own, I responded badly, with aggression. 'What the fuck do they know? What would they ever understand,' I'd say to myself. Everybody seemed a bit lame and weak. Which is obviously a horrible way to think.

Then, over time, I saw that this wasn't a challenge to me; it was an opportunity. All these people, who had skills I didn't have, who had life experiences I didn't have, who saw the world in a completely way – I realised I could grab everything I wanted from them.

That was so fucking exciting, because it was another liberation. I stopped seeing change as something restrictive or frightening. Instead, I realised it's one of the most positive tools there is, something that gives you the chance to develop and grow at a pace you never would have dreamed of before.

CHANGE IS ALWAYS POSSIBLE

Recently I had forty-five minutes to kill before a carol service for the Royal Marine cadets, so I decided to pop into one of two pubs that are opposite Portsmouth Cathedral for a coffee. When I put my head through the door of the first I saw immediately that it was full of navy personnel who were a) mostly dressed in Christmas jumpers, and b) mostly pissed.

There wasn't even a decision to make. I headed over to the second place, which was almost completely empty. The navy guys weren't being too rowdy, they were just people having fun – but that wasn't the point. I knew that there was minimal chance of anything positive coming out of any time I spent there. Sure, if I'd wanted to get on the beers and spend the evening with them, it would probably have been brilliant. That afternoon, however, I just wanted a quiet coffee. The first pub was not the place I needed to be in. I didn't want to be dragged around or grabbed for selfies, and I knew I'd have reacted badly. And something worse *might* have happened. Within seconds I'd assessed what the outcome was more likely to be. This is what I do all the time. Is it more likely to be negative than positive? Boom, I'm out of there.

Four or five years ago my attitude would have been different. Much more, 'Oh! A bit of liveliness. Love that!' If you'd have told me six years ago that I wouldn't be out drinking every weekend with the lads, I'd have thought you were mad. I'd have said, 'Nah, that's just me, that's my DNA. I love to go out, I love to get in fights.' If you'd told me that real men walk away from fights, I'd have told you that you were talking bollocks. Back then, the idea that I could change, even if I wanted to, would have seemed impossible.

But you don't have to stay the same. It's so easy to convince yourself that aspects of your behaviour are an innate part of you – that you're naturally lazy, or unlucky; that you can't help getting into scraps. That's such a negative way of looking at the world. It robs you of power and of the chance to become the best possible version of yourself.

I was lucky that going to prison allowed me to step outside my immediate circumstances and take a proper look at my life. Sitting in my cell, I could see things so much more clearly. You don't need to get banged up to make that distance for yourself. Try to imagine that you're meeting yourself for the first time. Be brutally honest. What aspects of your personality and behaviour would you change if you could? The very act of asking that question is the first step. As soon as you realise that another version of yourself is possible, the idea of making incremental improvements, which might once have appeared inconceivable, suddenly feels as if it's within your grasp.

Emilie

When Anthony told me he'd decided to leave the military I
thought, 'Yes, now is the time.' What neither of us knew was
how hard it would be for both of us to adjust. Anthony has talked
elsewhere about the struggles he faced, and I saw how much
he went through in those months, but it was tough for me too. I
wasn't in the forces, and yet I lived on the married patch and, in
almost as many ways as Anthony, my life was consumed by the
military.

It wasn't just that it was the military that determined when I
got to see my husband, where he travelled to, where we lived. It
was more mundane stuff: they paid all of our bills out of his
wages. It seems minor, and yet at the same time it wasn't at all.
Our rent in the military was silly; outside we suddenly realised
how expensive it was just to get by. The demands civilian life
was making on us seemed oppressive because we weren't used
to it. We'd left this unbelievably protected bubble and were now
trying to make our way without anyone to show us how.

My whole married life had been in the military. I knew nothing
else. We'd been safe there (who's going to burgle a military

camp?), and I knew I could trust and rely on my neighbours. They were my friends, and they understood everything implicitly – they were in exactly the same position. Then we were out, all of that protection fell away, and suddenly we both felt vulnerable.

Maybe if Anthony had found his feet sooner we'd have been OK. But he didn't. For the first months after leaving the military he was as lost as I've ever seen him. I'd tell him how unfair his behaviour was. I wasn't going out because I knew that somebody had to look after the children. I'm the one up all night worried sick, you're the one who crashes home at silly o'clock and then spends the next day sleeping off a hangover. And, worse, I'd have to pretend to the kids that everything was great and normal when inside I was screaming.

All he'd say was that it was never his fault. That didn't cut it for me.

Then the moment came when I was woken at three in the morning by somebody hammering on my door. It was a friend of his who'd been with him that night. He asked to come in, explaining that he needed to talk to me about Anthony. He explained what had happened. To begin with, all I thought was, 'Here we go again.' Then, suddenly, it hit me that something was different this time round. You don't do something like that and walk away with a little slap on the wrist. My husband was in deep trouble.

The more I learned about what had gone on, the more I was surprised by how out of character for him it had been to act like that towards someone in authority. The weird thing was that the times he'd got arrested before, the thing the police involved would always say was how lovely and polite Anthony had been. (I know, I know.) Something that night must have triggered him. Still, I agreed with his punishment. You just don't do that kind of thing. Plain as day.

The day I got back from court I was alone. The children were with my mum and I went into our eerily silent living room and poured myself a glass of wine. I'm not much of a drinker, but it felt appropriate. I just sat there, looking out of the window, thinking, 'What the fuck am I going to do?' For some reason I'd expected him to be there with me. Instead, he was in a prison cell. My sisters, parents and one friend were the only other people that knew. That mood stayed with me until the next morning when I woke up and decided to carry on as close to normal as I could. I was determined that the only person who'd be affected by it would be me. It was five months, I knew I could hide it. I never took the kids to see him. I took extra hours and used up all our savings. Somehow we survived. Had it been any longer, I don't know if I'd have been able to keep it up. I'm so glad this wasn't put to the test.

Anthony was worried about me, of course he was. But what could he do? I dealt with his problems, I dealt with mine. That's how it had to be.

LESSONS

Change shakes the world around you up. Most of the time you can't stop that process, but you can make sure that you're on hand to pick up all of the positives that emerge. Learn to see change as a process that opens up new spaces for you to dive into.

Don't be afraid of cutting ties. We get too attached to some things that, when we've got the time and space to really reflect on them, we find were actually holding us back.

Change offers you the chance to diversify your thinking. It's another route to becoming the best version of yourself you can be.

It's OK to hit rock bottom. If I didn't have negativity in my life, I wouldn't know what positivity was. If you're not willing to plunge into fear, or uncertainty, you won't reap the rewards of coming out the other side.

When somebody tells you that you've changed, take it as a compliment. Personal change is always possible. You're not condemned to behave in a particular way for the rest of your life. Embrace change as a liberation, and make sure you carry on trying to change until the day that you die.

CHAPTER 6

MAKE MANY PLATFORMS

AFRICA. FOR SO long, the word alone was enough to get me excited. When I was a kid, it just held this allure for me. My head was filled with jungles and deserts, and people living what I saw as unbelievably exotic lives. And then I'd look at the empty French fields I'd dragged myself past a million times, and the tidy rows of shops and cafés that were the drab backdrop to my dull existence, and I'd wish there was some way I could be transported there.

That, it turned out, was one of the things that the military was really good at. If you're a lively personality who wants to see the world, there are many worse organisations you can join. They first sent me to Africa, to Sierra Leone, in 2006 with 40 Commando on a Short-term Training Team (STTT). The plan was to spend two six-week rotations in the country, passing on what they knew about jungle warfare and fieldcraft: tracking; how to catch, kill and cook a goat; how to set and site booby-traps; how to find or catch water in the jungle, and then how to purify it. It was my first experience of soldiering in a drastically different environment.

I'd never been to the jungle before, and so I was buzzing ahead of the trip.

We flew into an airport the size of a garden shed. The first thing that hit us was the heat. You step out of the air-conditioned cocoon of the plane onto the tarmac and then, boom. Your eyes struggle to adjust to a light more dazzling than anything you've experienced before. It was as if tropical Africa was looked over by a different, far hotter sun. And then you feel the heat gripping your body. It's so intense that at times it's like you're being squeezed by it, like the heat possessed an actual physical existence.

It took a few moments before I was capable of registering anything else. Then I began to notice other things: the presence of the rich red dust that covered every still surface and the absence of all the things you were used to seeing at airports. No duty-free, no shops, no checks. We're all so accustomed to travelling through extra-heightened security systems, having guards go through every corner of your baggage. In Freetown I wasn't sure if anybody was even looking at passports.

I remember thinking: right, we're in Africa now. Things are going to be different.

It's hard to get your bearings. To begin with, it can seem as if everybody wants to be your friend. It's only after you've been there for a while that you can start spotting when there's an ulterior motive – that the guy who's come up to you in the street is actually only being nice to you because he wants something from you, that he just sees you as a rich English guy. And, to be fair, that's how you feel too. Early on I remember getting out a million leones, which was worth about £200. It was mental.

It didn't take long for me to fall in love with the country itself. In theory, we weren't allowed out of the compound we were staying in except to go to a few places that were considered safe. There was a casino, for instance, and that was fine, but if you came out of it and went the wrong way you'd pretty quickly find yourself in all sorts of trouble. More than one of the lads that I went out there with thought it would be a good idea to chip off by themselves to some of the beach bars that we'd been told to avoid. They'd arrive back later the same night having lost their wallet, their watch and a fair amount of their pride.

You need to remember that in 2006 Sierra Leone wasn't the holiday destination it has since become. Things were still raw there as they'd only just emerged from an unimaginably brutal civil war. The country had seen terrible things – brainwashed, drug-addicted child soldiers hacking limbs off prisoners with machetes; people being burned alive after having been locked in their houses – and a society that had been brought to its knees was only just beginning to pick itself up again.

I was lucky. I never had any trouble. People were nice to me and I was nice back, and I think it broke their guard down. Once you start talking to people, going on nights out with guys from the Sierra Leone military, you see a different side. They took me to all the black markets. You had to be careful there – one guy I knew spent a grand on what he thought was a huge uncut diamond; it was only once he got back that he realised it was just a lump of glass – but if you stayed sharp and didn't let greed cloud your judgement, it was lots of fun.

I enjoyed the work too. There are long-standing connections between the two countries; we've trained their military for years. They like us there and want to form relationships – they know it might lead to opportunities. You could say it was a bit like networking. But I didn't really have my eye on making anything out of the time I spent in the country. As far as I was concerned it was a great experience to have under my belt, although I was aware that just the fact of being there opened the door to the sorts of relationships that wouldn't have been possible if I'd been on a normal deployment.

I was a lance corporal at the time, doing a full corporal's job, and over the months I was out there I made friends with a colonel in the Sierra Leonean army. I'd have these fascinating conversations with him about diamonds, but I never thought anything would come of it. I was just interested in him and all the things he had to tell me. Because he was a colonel he could take me everywhere, from the office of the minister of transport to the shanty bars that were supposed to be off-limits. So, even though I was in uniform, I was OK. I got to know the people.

Despite hearing my fair share of horror stories, I didn't allow the negativity to affect my own reactions when we went out. My attitude was: it hasn't happened to me and, until it does, I'll enjoy life. I knew that some of the people I encountered probably had it in their heads that they might try to rob me, but I tried not to let it infect the way I interacted with them. When they all crowded round me, I could have reacted badly and pushed them away or started shouting, which would probably have meant that I *would* get robbed. Instead, I just made a joke of it. 'Hey, hey, what's going on here? Are you trying to fight me? What's in your pockets?' Mucking around. Not showing any discomfort. Being friendly and positive.

I'm the same when I meet people anywhere. You know how it is. Before you're introduced to someone, there'll be loads of other people chipping in, saying, 'Oh, he's this, he's that.' It's not that I ignore what I'm told – I'll always keep it at the back of my mind – but I don't let it cloud my own impressions. I'm the one who's going to determine how I feel about a person, not somebody else chatting away in my ear.

You'll never hear me badmouth somebody. It's not that I don't have opinions. I do, strong ones. There are plenty of people who I think are utter pricks, but really, is there any positive outcome, to anybody, to spilling your guts like that? Much better, if somebody asks you about somebody else who you don't really like, to just say, 'Well, he's not my cup of tea.'

The way I see it, if you let decisions be governed by other people's negativity, you'll end up living life in a cage. More than that, if you write someone off, you might also be writing off an opportunity that might end up being to your advantage. Just because someone else has an opinion, why should you feel obliged to share it? Trust your instincts. It's your mind, so why would you let somebody else make it up for you?

My time in Sierra Leone was one big adventure. I was excited to meet new people and interact with the locals, and I very quickly felt at home. It was helpful being a soldier, as they love their military out there. They're proud of them, and rightly so; they're good at what they do. And precisely because memories of the civil war are still so vivid in their minds, they also remember the big role the British military played in bringing peace to the country. When they found out I was in the Marines, who'd formed part of the force we sent out there as part of Operation Palliser, they were like, 'Oh wow, you guys are on our side.'

In their eyes, either you were there to get on with them, spend money in the community, give something back; or you were one of the thousands of Westerners they'd seen come and go over the decades, including men who were only interested in the country's minerals, who didn't want to know anything about the culture and wanted to get out as quickly as they could. When I headed out to the bars on the other side of town, I was pleased to see that they saw me in the former camp. If I'd just been a random white guy who'd gone out there hoping to get rich by buying and selling diamonds, I'd probably have come back without any fingers.

They really embraced me, and I embraced them back. I got into their culture and food, eating with my fingers, and joking and laughing with their families. I even picked up Krio, the local creole language, which mashes up English with words from all over the place. My view is that you should always try to blend into the situation. It's not about changing who you are, it's just adapting to your environment, putting on different masks to fit the company you're in. You can't go into situations with a narrow mind; you have to be humble and open yourself up to every single possibility. If you tell yourself that something's going to be shit, then, guess what, you'll probably have a shit time. When you find something interesting – whether it's a place, a person or an activity – respond to it, play up to it, make it work for you. Get every single thing you possibly can out of it.

They used to call me '*Oporto*' at the beginning, which basically means 'nice white man'. It was a hangover from the days when the Portuguese had been in Sierra Leone, and was half affectionate, half derogatory. It all depended on the context they used it in. After a while they started to call me '*Salambobo*', local boy. I fucking buzzed off that.

The thing I loved most was how uncomplicated life was there. Yeah, lots of people were poor, living in tiny corrugated huts in shanty towns, but they seemed happy. They'd reduced existence to the essentials – food, friends, laughter. Another thing that really attracted me to Sierra Leone was its lawlessness. There aren't many rules governing what you can and can't do, or who you can and can't be. At least, there's nothing in writing. Everything's about informal connections. There's no bureaucracy – it's pure personal interaction. If you're a social animal, you get on.

That looseness and spontaneity was intoxicating, even when it bordered on criminality. It's easy to bribe people out there. Actually, in lots of situations it's *expected*. So many of the interactions are greased with a bit of cash. If you wave a hundred-dollar bill in the faces of a passport official, or the guy from the government in charge of visas, they think all of their Christmases have come at once.

I wouldn't say Sierra Leone is unique in its attitude to this sort of thing. Europe's probably more corrupt than Africa in lots of ways, but in the West it's swept under the carpet, or carried out by big corporations when nobody's looking. In Sierra Leone it was much more open, a bit more like a game. And, very often, the people that got on the wrong side of their criminal enterprises probably had it coming.

They've got the biggest scams going out there, and they're amazing at what they do. You hear about those Nigerian email guys, but the men behind the Sierra Leonean diamond cons are something else. Hanging around with the locals, drinking beers and chatting with them about the stuff that they'd seen – or been involved in themselves – I realised that it's all properly organised out there, and that the men running things are not to be fucked with.

I spent so many nights sitting in a bar, watching as an English guy with fifty grand wedged in his pocket walked in looking all cocky, his greed dripping from him like sweat, and got ushered into a little room round the back. You'd just know what was about to happen. The police would pile in and the next you'd see of him he'd be lying on the floor, shaking. He'd have been really shitted up with all sorts of threats about what might happen to white boys who've got themselves mixed up in illegal diamond trading, and the police would soon very gently offer to help solve the problem by escorting him to the airport and onto the next flight home.

It's pure greed and sense of entitlement. They would have been told about 50,000-carat parcels of diamonds. But these don't exist unless you're Tiffany or De Beers – certainly not if you're a bottom-feeder like them.

The more advanced scams, which targeted far more sophisticated and richer marks, would unfold over a number of days, and several locations. Early on, after the requisite amount of wining and dining, the mark would be brought to a proper government office where the gemologist they had with them could inspect the merchandise, which would be absolutely legit. Then the diamonds would be parcelled up, sealed, stamped. They'd get their certificates. It was this amazing charade. Everything looked above board. If you were watching the process you'd be so impressed by how transparent and honest everyone involved was. At every stage they'd be offering the buyer the chance to inspect what was happening.

The problem was, you could have the best gemologist in the world and they'd find nothing wrong. But it was the wrong sort of knowledge. The key fact was that there were probably only four people in the whole country who had the authority to issue an export licence, and these guys doing the scams, they ain't it. The diamonds the marks walked out of the office with were kosher, it was the papers that were the problem. They looked absolutely perfect and yet they were worthless.

The scammers have got people working for them in airports around the world. So the mark will head to the airport, thinking they've got everything sewn up, and then when they get there and their bags are searched, it's suddenly: 'What's all this? What *have* you got here? Are you *smuggling* diamonds?' And they'll protest and wave their papers, and it won't make any difference at all.

First they'll be arrested, and the diamonds confiscated. The diamonds will head back across town, and they end up in the same drawer of the same office that they started the day in, ready to be used next time. The Englishman will be hurled into a little shitty dark cell, stripped down to their underwear and given a choice. 'We can keep you here, put you through the system, charge you with diamond smugg—.' This is usually the moment when the new prisoner lets out a big gasp; it's very rare that the policeman will ever need to finish the sentence. 'Or,' he'll say, far more friendly now, 'you can put your clothes on, get on the next flight out of Sierra Leone, and never come back here again.' As far as I know, nobody's ever taken their chances in a trial.

It's possible to take the scam even further. I know of one case where some French dealers got their export licences OK and even had plenty of time to knock back the champagne on the flight home to Paris. That was where the jaws of the trap slammed shut on them. They got arrested as soon as they got off the plane in France, and very naturally they blamed the guy who issued them with their licence. Back the diamonds went into their drawer in that little government office. The Frenchmen were told that the licence guy would be punished back in Sierra Leone. The victims might have had their freedom, but they no longer had their diamonds, or the million dollars they'd paid as a deposit, and nor were the Sierra Leonean authorities – who were of course in on the scam themselves – ever going to let them back into the country so that they could try to recover the money.

It's clean. It's cold-blooded. I saw all of this happening, but because there was this perception that I was in the military and giving something back, I wasn't in any danger. In fact, it got to the point where people trusted me so much that they wanted to get me involved in the really big scams;

the 'deals' where millions of pounds were at stake. In their eyes, I was the perfect man to tempt greedy Englishmen. That, clearly, was never going to happen – I'm not sure it would have gone down too well if anyone in authority had discovered that one of their lance corporals was mixed up in a diamond con. Still, it was flattering in a weird way.

The tour finished, I went back to the UK and didn't give it another thought until a few years later when I saw a job advert that an American company had put up on a military message board. There's lots of work out there for people willing to do it. Lots of governments willing to pay good money for things they can't, or won't, do themselves. I've done work for the Ivory Coast and Burundi. This particular post was looking for men who had experience as snipers to go out to Sierra Leone and help train their army's newly created sniper unit. I put in for it, got the job, and as soon as I did, I ran through my contacts and dug out the colonel's number.

A couple of nights after I arrived I met up with the colonel, and he hooked me up with his nephew Julius (I say 'nephew' – everybody out there had hundreds of nephews and uncles and so on, so there's a fighting chance he wasn't a blood relation at all). When I first met Julius I was doing a pool workout in my hotel. Suddenly this huge silhouette appeared, almost blocking the light out, and I thought, 'Who's this lunatic here?' I didn't pay him much attention, cracked on with my routine, and it was only when I finished and the colonel joined us that we were properly introduced. Almost as soon as he'd appeared, the colonel dashed off to do some business of his own, leaving Julius and me to chat. We really clicked.

Julius is a big guy and always reminds me of the rapper Rick Ross. He's bubbly, full of personality, always joking around and unbelievably charismatic. Julius's mum is English, his dad used to be Sierra Leone's minister of finance, so he was unbelievably well connected. He seemed to know everyone, from bar owners right up to the country's attorney general.

His family's connections with the UK mean that he grew up floating between the two countries. He's as at home here as is he is walking around in his smart T-shirts and expensive trainers in Sierra Leone. We started hanging out together all the time. By day I'd be training snipers and by night I'd hanging around with Julius, going to the beach bars.

Just as when I'd been there the first time, I had to be careful going to certain parts of Freetown. There were some bars where they'd probably never seen a white man. I wasn't ever fazed by it, and in fact there was only one time we had any trouble. We'd gone to the other side of town, which probably was a bit more edgy. Julius had warned me that I might get a bit of shit, but I wasn't overly bothered.

As we entered the bar, every face in it turned towards us and the room went quiet, as if our existence alone was a shock. The silence didn't last for long. Soon we had guys coming up to us saying that we had to leave. Right now. Obviously, there was no way I was moving. I wasn't going to let them walk all over me like that. Most bars had a couple of security lads lurking unobtrusively in one of their corners. This place was no different. We went over and slipped them a couple of $20 notes. Normally this would have been enough to buy us a bit of peace. Not here, it turned out.

Another guy came up to me. 'You're not welcome here.' I tried to defuse the situation by offering him a beer. 'No, I don't want your beer,' he said, pushing himself closer to me. He was a big guy, he probably had a foot on me, and I could smell the alcohol on his breath and the sweat from his body. 'Look,' I told him, still trying to be reasonable, 'I've offered you a beer. Get out of my face.' He didn't move an inch. Then he gave me a shove in the chest. I held my ground.

Out of the corner of my eye I could see the security guard I thought we'd paid off. Rather than protecting us, as he was supposed to, he was just watching, like the situation had nothing to do with him. Fine, I thought, it seems as if I'll have to look after myself. The guy shoved me in the chest again. Harder this time. Then again. Right, I told myself, if he does it *one* more time then he's getting the good news. He went to push me, but this time I took a step back, which momentarily knocked him off balance. Whack. My fist smashed into his face and a second later he'd hit the deck.

The room erupted. All of this guy's mates came over and I disappeared under a pile of enraged Sierra Leoneans. Julius had been about eight metres away while all this was unfolding. As soon as he saw I was in trouble he rampaged over, like an angry elephant. He'd been a promising rugby player when he was younger, and it showed. Pow! Pow! Pow! People were bouncing off him left right and centre. And he was moving fast. I had no idea he could shift that quickly.

The second he reached me, leaving a trail of bruised and bewildered men in his wake, the whole bar went quiet again. You could see everyone in there was just staring at me and Julius, taking in his bulk and the tattoos on my arms. When we'd walked in they must have thought he was a soft businessman who'd grown up abroad, and I was his white friend. It was clear they were dealing with something pretty different.

As we slowly finished our beers, the security guards seemed to remember what they were paid to do, picking the guy I'd punched off the floor and tossing him out of the bar. At about the same time we decided that we'd probably shown enough defiance for one evening, and headed off into the night.

Before long, our evening conversations turned to the kinds of opportunities that might be on offer in Sierra Leone. That was when he mentioned diamonds. Because I'd already been accepted into the Sierra Leonean family, it was like it was them offering me the opportunity; I was different from all the white guys who came in year after year, who had no interest in the place except leaving richer than they'd arrived, and who, as a result, got scammed. It was a fuck of a lot more interesting than the security work I'd been doing up until then. Brilliant, I told Julius, count me in.

Our plan was that we'd raise some cash, buy some diamonds, cut and polish them, and then sell them on. Any profit we'd split 50–50. There are two ways you can do business. You can export them with a Kimberley Certificate, which is the documentation you need to prove that they're not blood diamonds. The other, more risky, route is if you've got contacts at the airport who can escort you through without any paperwork. We did a bit of both.

I'd go back to the UK and raise money, either from friends or businessmen, and then return to Sierra Leone. For a while almost nobody else knew I was out there. There was a real freedom to it. I could operate on my own terms. When things went wrong, I knew I only had myself to blame. And it made it easier to disentangle everything in the aftermath. I could see where stuff had gone wrong, and draw the lessons from it accordingly.

Our investors in Britain would put in an order for, say, 150 carats' worth of diamonds. Then Julius would go out and pick them. Next we'd take them to Antwerp to be cut and polished, before we carried them over to the UK. The whole thing took six weeks. If you'd given me £100,000 to buy the diamonds, you'd comfortably double that on the process as a whole. We took a fee on each transaction.

There was no danger we were going to become millionaires – when it comes down to it, you're bringing back rough diamonds that look like stones, and so you'll lose 50 per cent in the cutting and polishing process – but things were good, and getting better as we went on.

And then Ebola kicked off. British Airways cancelled all flights out of Sierra Leone. I was supposed to be going back home for my cousin's wedding, but it didn't look like I was going to be able to make it. Not ideal, but I could cope. Then, with the disease spreading at a vicious rate, there was a three-day ban on anybody leaving their homes, and anybody with Ebola, or who was even suspected of having it, was put in quarantine. The alarming thing about this was that the initial symptoms of Ebola aren't too different to the symptoms of malaria and the flu. So if you walked out of your door with a runny nose, you were fucked.

Things got worse when the government starting setting up checkpoints along the roads. All the roads from the diamond mines into Freetown were suddenly vulnerable. The guys manning the checkpoints knew where the trucks bringing the jewels into the city had come from, so they'd stop them, jam a thermometer in the mouths of the men in the trucks, and, surprise, surprise, 'Oh, we're going to need to bring you in for tests.'

By the time they got back to their vehicles, their money, diamonds and anything else of any value at all would be gone. So the whole operation shuts down. The scammers were getting scammed.

We had presidential passes that should in theory have allowed us to move around without being harassed, but Ebola had turned everything upside down. It wasn't worth the hassle, as we'd reached the point where the potential negatives had started to outweigh the potential positives. This meant that we encountered a new problem. We'd a lot of money held in Sierra Leonean accounts. You can leave it for a little while, fine, but the longer the cash sits there, the greater the chance that something might happen to it.

In December I heard that there weren't going to be any direct flights back to Britain until the new year. The outlook was bleak. I had to get home, but I was stuck in Freetown, with no obvious way out. The only option was to do a sort of daisy chain of flights over two and a half days: Sierra Leone to Senegal; Senegal to Cape Verde; Cape Verde to Madrid; Madrid to London. Legally speaking, you're supposed to have a visa to get into Senegal. A visa I did not have. But they have different rules in Africa. Actually, they pretty much have no rules; that's why I love the place. We drew on all of our diamond connections to make sure we got escorted through Freetown airport like VIPs, then we got to passport control in Senegal.

I handed my passport over to the guy behind the desk. He took his time, looking at the photo, looking back up at me. Then he started flicking through, before looking up.

'You've got no visa.'

'The visa's on the front page, sir.'

He turned to the front page. Our eyes met. And then, almost in the same movement, he flicked the hundred-dollar bill I'd put there earlier onto his lap and, bang bang bang, stamped my document.

I've not been back since. This was partly because the right opportunities didn't come up, partly because Emilie suggested it was time to lead a more sustainable, less haphazard life, one where I wasn't always looking over my shoulder. And also because, not long after, I got the call from the *Who Dares Wins* producers. Everything changed after that. I was ready, so ready, for something new. It's not always clear which of the opportunities you encounter are the ones that are going to help lift you up to the stratosphere, and which are going to lead you down a cul-de-sac. In this case, it was overwhelming obvious. That chance came up, and I grabbed it with every fucking fibre of my body.

OPPORTUNITIES ARE ALWAYS
AROUND THE CORNER

I love being on this planet. I see it as a positive, fascinating place that just teems with possibilities. I'll seize all the opportunities that come my way, see them out to the end and tie them together. I know that even if nine of them end up going nowhere, the tenth will work. You don't want to be in the position where you look back and think, 'Fucking hell, that's the one opportunity I wished I'd jumped on.' That regret can eat you up.

You have to be hungry, and committed too, but most of all you need that positivity that will keep you going through those days when it isn't immediately obvious that your hard work is going to pay off. I find that so often you'll dismiss an encounter you've had with somebody that went nowhere, or a project you entered into that became a dead end, only to find out later on that in fact, without realising it, you were laying the groundwork for an opening in the future. Don't panic if you can't work it out straight away – its time will come. It might take ten years before the seed you planted flowers and presents you with an opportunity.

I didn't realise that the time I'd spent chatting about diamonds with the colonel during my first posting in Sierra Leone would come to anything. But that's the thing about having a positive mindset; it guarantees that something new and exciting is always waiting around the corner for you, as long as you're willing to go out into the world and find it.

LOOK AT THE WORLD FROM THE INSIDE OUT

If you understand yourself, you'll find a way of achieving your goals that feels natural. Things will fall into place of their own accord. If you're relying on other people's ambitions – and if you haven't made sense of yourself and don't know yourself – you'll always end up trying to force the wrong pieces into the wrong jigsaw, and end up feeling frustrated. You'll have this sense of wanting to make something work, because somebody has told you that it's the right career path for you, but not really knowing why, or how.

If you don't know yourself, if you're not being honest with yourself, you won't recognise those crucial moments when the right opportunity emerges. You won't get that energy connection. If you look at the world from the inside out, if you're honest with yourself, if you follow stuff that excites you and maybe scares you a little – those moments that spark your body into going, 'Woah, this is cool, get ready, get ready, get ready' – things will make sense and will naturally fall into place.

MAKE IT YOU

I get told by people that I got a lucky break being offered a role on *SAS: Who Dares Wins*. All the time.

So I say to them, 'Do you know what the show's about?'

'Yeah, ex-Special Forces training people.'

'Well, how do you think I got into that job? Do you think it might have anything to do with the thirteen years I spent in the military? My time in the Paras, Marines and Special Forces? All the hardcore missions I went on? Or do you think it all just fell into my lap?'

I didn't realise it at the time, of course, but everything I did from the age of sixteen was a preparation for the moment that this opportunity was offered to me. The reason I was able to recognise it for the chance it was when I got the call from the TV producers was because of my positive attitude.

There were a lot of guys like me floating around the project when it was first mooted. And then when the Ministry of Defence told us we had to stay away from it, every single one of them scattered back into the shadows, except for me and Foxy. If other people wanted to hide under their rocks, fine, but I knew it was an opportunity and there was no fucker who was going to stop me from grabbing it with both hands.

Now, of course, they all want to be involved, but that train's long gone, mate. You never want to be left in a position where you're bitter because you're watching other people do well and all you can think is, 'That should have been me.' Make it you.

One mistake people make all the time is waiting for the BIG opportunity to come along. Opportunities fly by their face every day, but they don't take them. What they should be doing is grabbing all the smaller opportunities that come their way. It's a bit like those people who are so convinced that there's only one soulmate out there for them in the world that they reject any other partner. How will you know that the 'one' *is* the 'one'? And what if you realised too late that the heartbreaks and messy endings that everybody goes through are actually the only way you can properly prepare for a relationship you hope will last for the rest of your life. What this sort of thinking gets so wrong is that it promotes the idea that opportunities are just hanging over our heads, waiting to drop into our laps. No. You have to be positive, go out there and *make* your own opportunities. You cannot just sit back and hope they'll come your way.

If you haven't practised reeling small fish in, how are you going to cope when you finally hook the big one?

There will be situations in life when you realise you've let something potentially valuable slip through your hands – a job you should have applied for, a trip you should have taken. These are the moments when you have to move on as quickly as possible. Learn whatever lessons you can from the experience, but don't waste time hoping that somehow you'll get another chance or beat yourself up about it. If the train's gone, the train's gone. The only thing to do is to make sure that next time you don't miss the train. Make another platform. Make as many platforms as you can. It's a numbers game, so get the numbers to work in your favour.

ACTIVITY CREATES OPPORTUNITY

I hear lots of people complain about work, as if it's something that gets in the way of their real plans, but for me it's the best form of therapy. It teaches you discipline; it keeps you sharp.

This is true whether you're bar staff in a grotty pub or the CEO of a tech company. You've got to get there on time, you've got tasks to work through, you're interacting with fellow workers and outside customers. The more you work, the more opportunities come your way.

I remember a doorman I met recently at a lunch on Berkeley Square. As he opened the door, he gasped with excitement.

'Ant Middleton! I've got all of your books! I've got one in my bag right now. I can't believe it. Will you sign it?' He told me that four months ago he was on the verge of self-harming, but that reading my books had changed his life. 'How do you do it?' he asked me. 'How do you stay so positive?'

'Well, by doing the same thing as you are now.'

'What do you mean?'

'These doors you've just opened. How many times a day do you reckon you do it?'

'Hundreds, maybe close to a thousand.'

'OK, and what opportunities have come up today?'

'You walking in! It meant I could meet you, get you to sign your book.'

'So what do you carry on doing?'

'Keep opening these doors?'

'Exactly that. You've got an opportunity now because you're working. You might think it's mundane, but did you get here on time?'

'Yep.'

'And the more regular customers you see and impress with the sort of sharpness you've shown me today, the more opportunities you'll get.'

Everyone thinks that opportunities fall out of the sky, and that suddenly you'll go from zero to a hundred. But opportunities don't exist outside of context. What's going to open things up for you is you grafting away, day after day, showing people that you've got a spark about you, you're good at talking to people, take care of the way you present yourself. That's what happened to me in Sierra Leone. The fact that I was open and hard-working and made the time to speak to the colonel ensured that when I called him up years after I'd first met him, he was massively up for helping me out.

You'll never know what the opportunity is until it arrives. All you can do is make yourself the best version of yourself that you can so that when the moment arrives, you can seize it. Take what inspiration you can from everybody you meet, learn what you can – the fact that so many people cross your path means you're in the perfect position for that.

Challenge yourself on a daily basis, look for chances to increase your positivity or to be inspired by others – whether that's just somebody that's made you smile or has taught you something valuable. They're all gifts, and life is about learning to recognise them. A lot of people make the mistake of thinking that they can only learn things from great writers or leaders or people who are famous for some reason. Great, they probably can inspire you; just don't forget to look to the people around you as well. Just the process of searching on its own will keep your mind stimulated.

When I was a sniper spending days at a time getting wet and cold, shitting in a bag, watching, watching, watching, even though it could seem as if nothing was happening and that nothing would ever happen, I never switched off. For lots of people, sniping is a sort of glamorous, one-shot, one-kill affair. Nine times out of ten it's information-gathering. There's no excitement, no glory. It's excruciatingly dull. It's not about getting headshots, it's about maintaining disciplined, discreet communication with a fire team.

I remained motivated because I knew that that my main motivator was positive. Whoever our target was, whether they were an IED-maker or whatever, I knew we were trying – ultimately – to deter evil. If you've found that positive motivator, then it will help you get through almost anything. The other thing that kept me from losing my mind was that on those days when nothing seemed to be going on, I didn't just switch off to emptiness. I kept my mind engaged. I was always trying to second-guess what might happen next. I might have been sitting there watching a compound so that I could provide a positive ID on a particular individual whom we suspected was operating out of there. And although it might have been empty for that moment, I tried to create a complete image in my mind. I filled it with potential problems. I thought about the children there who didn't see anything strange about the weapon-laden vehicles being brought into their home.

I could have written everything off that wasn't 'action'. Instead, I kept my mind active like that and became so hyper-focused that I was able to notice even the tiniest of details through my scope: a notepad that's been left on a table in the compound. The more you look at something, the more you *see*.

Hard work brings opportunity in its wake. People will notice your dedication. Don't try to figure life out while you're doing nothing – it's much better to try to do that tricky work when you're doing something. Never think you're too good to collect glasses or start from the bottom. How do you know that just being there won't put you in the right place at the right time?

STAY AWAY FROM THE GREEN-EYED MONSTER

Envy will only ever drain you. It stops you from seeing either your strengths or your weaknesses clearly, and is one of the most negative traits I can imagine – a massive, corrosive distraction. You're always on edge and you lose your ability to focus on who you are, what you need to do, what your goals are, where your path is. Envy makes you want to be somebody you're not. Instead of existing in the moment, all you can see is what the other person has. When you should be focusing on your life, all you can think about is theirs.

You can and should learn from others, taking inspiration from them whenever you can, but don't ever think it's a good idea to try to actually imitate another human being. Even if you might be able to squeeze 90 per cent of yourself into another skin, you'll never be able to inhabit it fully. Rather than giving yourself the chance to become the best version of yourself, you'll end up as a poundshop version of someone else.

The worst thing you can do is to let envy spill out into malicious behaviour. I've felt envy before, but I've never slagged people off, or talked them down to make myself feel better. That's the emptiest of victories. If nothing else, it won't always have the impact you want. I know that when people badmouth me, I *love* it. It gives me so much more energy, inspiration and determination to show them how wrong they are.

It's no use pretending that there won't be moments in your life when you're affected by envy. It can sweep through us when we least expect it. But if you can't stop it entirely, you can at least learn to recognise it for what it is and see if there's anything within this negative that you can turn into a positive. Are you able to use the feeling that envy provokes to fuel you? If there's a friend that has a nicer house than you, don't waste time resenting them for it. Use it as a driver to inspire you to work harder at your job, or look for a new, better one. If someone at work has been given a promotion that you thought you deserved, envy makes it too easy to avoid being honest with yourself. Instead of lashing out, ask yourself what they were doing that you weren't. You might not like the answer you get, but if you're willing to learn from the experience, you'll soon find a way of turning that negative into a positive.

Envy also leads to greed, which distorts your motives. It makes you willing to do anything for material gain. Instead of doing good things to attain a good goal, you'll be doing bad things to attain a bad goal. Your aim should be to become the best version of yourself. If you achieve this, then it's likely that material gain will follow. When you get greedy you get this the wrong way round. Greed is not sustainable; personal improvement is. All those British guys being mugged off by African scammers were the victims of their own greed. They wanted to take the easy way to riches without putting any proper work in first. Even if they'd succeeded in making a quick buck once, it would never be sustainable for them. And what would they have learned? Would they have picked up new skills or contacts? I very much doubt it.

Emilie

My nan is 101. She once told me that people give up on relationships too easily. You've got to fight for what you have. So many marriages fail in the forces; I was determined ours wouldn't be one of them. I knew what I'd signed up for when I married Anthony, and that didn't change when he went to prison.

What made this easier was that I've always believed he'd be successful at something, it's just that for quite a long time neither of us knew what that would be. I know the real Anthony, so when I see people saying, 'Oh, he beats up police officers,' all I think is, 'You don't even know him.' He had that desire to be a good family man, even during his wild days, but stuff hadn't quite clicked in place. I couldn't force that change, it had to be him. If somebody doesn't want to take a step forward, you can't force them.

It was while he was in prison that he properly committed to change. I really admired that about him. He knew when he looked around him that he was somewhere he didn't belong. He'd gone from being a member of the SBS, someone others looked up to, to a prisoner that people looked down on. I'll never forget how on one visit he turned to me and said. 'What am I doing here? This isn't me. I was in the Special Forces. How did I end up here?'

He promised my mum that he'd make something of himself. Most people would have said those words and then carried on as they had before. Anthony turned his life around.

He's always had this amazing energy and capacity for work. The only time Anthony is ever still is when he sleeps. The moment his eyes close, he's like a stone. The rest of the day he's like a blur of activity. When I first met him, he'd drive me mad the way he couldn't even watch TV without wriggling his foot or twitching his shoulder.

For a long time he hadn't really found a way of channeling all of this into something productive. That changed after prison. You could see he was more focused, more responsible. He worked and worked and worked, taking on jobs that he knew were potentially dangerous and that took him away from us. But he was only doing so because he knew he had to break free of his old circumstances and create new ones.

There were other qualities, aside from dedication, that helped him in this process. He's good at taking criticism on board. If you were to say to him, 'I'm not sure you handled that situation in the best way,' he'd listen. It's because he genuinely addicted to the idea of becoming the best version of himself. He sees criticism as useful, if it comes from the right person. Which is why he's not afraid to dish it out if he thinks it's justified.

Most of the time he's open to advice too, although it's not always immediately obvious. There will be occasions when I'll say something, maybe warn him against making a particular choice, and it'll look as if he's barely listened to me. Then, later on, he'll come back and say, 'I didn't do that because you advised me not to.'

All of this put together meant that when the right opportunities came up, he was in a good place to seize them. One thing led to another, and the prisoner who'd been so ashamed of the situation he'd found himself in had created an amazing career out of the rubble of his old existence.

I'm proud of the career that Anthony's made in the media, and I'm proud of the way he uses his platform to try to help people. But then I've *always* been proud of him. I was just as proud when he joined the Marines, just as proud when he came back from Afghanistan, just as proud when he passed selection into the SBS. I don't need to see his face on a TV screen to know what a good man he is. It annoys me that anybody would think he'd have to become famous for me to realise that.

LESSONS

Approach the world as a positive place. Don't fall into the trap of seeing it as aggressive and intimidating. The more you treat it as an environment that, sure, might have challenges, but is essentially welcoming and full of opportunities, the more you'll get out of life.

Overnight success is a false dream. Don't waste your existence waiting for that 'big' opportunity you think will come along and transform your life. What if it doesn't come? What if you don't recognise it when it does?

Move on, make new platforms. The moment you miss an opportunity is also the last minute you should ever think about that particular opportunity.

You can't just wait for opportunities to come to you. Go out into the world, meet people, do things. You'll be surprised what turns up.

Jealousy is the most negative of all the emotions. It'll tear up your life and make a mess of your priorities. Resist it with every bone in your body.

CHAPTER 7

YOU'VE GOT TO GO THROUGH THIS

IN THE WINTER of 2017 I had three days free, so when my mate Nims called and asked me if I wanted to climb the Matterhorn, I thought about it for approximately 0.05 seconds and then said, 'Fuck yes, when do we leave?'

Nims is a Special Forces operator, the first Gurkha to pass selection for the SBS. He joined the service about a year and a half after me, and as he was being given a bit of a hard time by some of the other guys, I took him under my wing. He's an excellent lad, and we've had a strong bond ever since.

On this occasion we thought we'd be a pair of Billy Big Bollockses and crack one of Europe's highest mountains at a time we knew nobody else would be trying to climb it. We'd been told – by more than one person – that it was really a summer route, but although we both were aware that it would be technical and challenging, we were also pretty confident it would be possible. 'No!' we said whenever anyone tried to persuade us otherwise, 'we *want* to be the only ones on the mountain.'

I'd completed some specialist mountain courses while in the military. I'd put these into practice in the mountains of Afghanistan and in the blizzards of Ben Nevis, I'd had training and I was with a trusted pal. Even though the Matterhorn has a reputation as one of the world's deadliest peaks – over five hundred people have been killed on its slopes since it was first climbed in 1865, and even now a handful of those who go up it each year never come back down – I was confident. And yet at the same time I could feel that tingle I get sometimes when I know something's going to be hard, maybe even take me out of my comfort zone. It's a mixture of fear and exhilaration; a sense that this new experience might open a door to somewhere even more exciting. I didn't know what the end result of this adventure would be, but I was 100 per cent into the idea of committing to it and finding out.

There wasn't much time to spare so we packed fairly lightly – there was a nagging voice at the back of my head that suggested maybe we'd packed too lightly – hopped on a plane and flew to Zurich, then travelled on to Zermatt. Everyone else we saw at the airport was in ski mode. They sat there with their excessively big bags of gear, looking smug in their oversized jackets, their faces with that red tinge you can only get from spending too much time on the slopes. You could just tell they were looking at us thinking, 'What are these jokers up to?' Which, when I look back on it *now*, was a pretty reasonable question.

The same thing happened later that day, when we visited the mountain guides' office. They were barely operational and it was clear that it was very much a seasonal affair. I could see that they were a bit shocked by what we were proposing to do. Their message was very much, 'Fill your boots, but just know we don't advise making any sort of attempt on the mountain – we can't take responsibility if anything goes wrong.'

Fine, we thought, as we made our own way up to the Hörnli Hut, a refuge at the foot of the mountain's north-east ridge. At least we know where we stand. The first sign that things were going to be tougher than we thought came pretty quickly. There were just a few flakes of snow to begin with, the sort you could just dust off your shoulder without much trouble. Then it started in earnest. Great swirls of the stuff billowed around us, getting heavier and heavier until we found ourselves in a complete white-out – you could barely see your hand in front of your face. Finally we staggered into the hut, relieved that we'd even managed to find it. We had been pretty boisterous earlier in the day, laughing and joking as if we were on a trip to the seaside. It was different now. Although neither of us were exactly worried, we were both far more alive to the scale of the task in front of us.

I began to understand the fear that this mountain had inspired in so many people for so long, and why it had remained unclimbed after many higher, more technical peaks had seen their first ascents during the golden age of alpinism in the Victorian era. There were times that night when I could not stop my mind from turning over stories I'd read about the fates of those who'd died on its slopes: mountaineers whose ropes had snapped while their comrades watched on helplessly, their bodies smashed to pieces on jagged outcrops of rock below. I realised how simple it would be for me to lose myself in a negative spiral and let this situation overwhelm me, so I worked hard to focus.

By the time we woke the next morning the snowfall had almost dropped off, but the wind had really picked up. It was lashing the mountain, whipping the freshly fallen snow up and into our faces, stinging any exposed flesh. There was something almost personal about the way it came again and again, never giving you even a second's respite.

Battered by the wind and labouring as we put one tired foot in front of the other, we climbed for an hour until we reached the point where our attack on the ridge was to begin in earnest. The thick snow that had fallen the day before completely obscured the route and the fixed ropes on the difficult pitches were buried by snow, meaning that the tricky moves would be particularly tense as we'd be soloing unroped. If we slipped, or lost our grip, that would be it. We'd join all the other poor souls who'd gone up the Matterhorn and never returned.

We approached the first steep pitch as steadily as we could, feeling carefully ahead of us, trying to put the weather out of our minds and concentrate only on the task in hand, but by now the wind had picked up considerably, as if it were preparing to escalate its attack on us. We pulled ourselves up closer to the edge. Then, with one last heave, we hoisted ourselves up over the sharp rocks. First there was a vicious screaming in our ears, followed by a feeling like being repeatedly punched in the face. It was relentless, absolutely relentless. I'd never experienced anything like it. Almost instantly we ducked down to avoiding being blasted anymore, and retreated down to a sheltered ledge to discuss the situation.

There was, it turned out, a good reason why we were alone up there. The atrocious winter weather. It should have been blindingly obvious to us even before we embarked on our attempt on the peak, but then everyone has 20/20 vision in hindsight. And not only were the harsh conditions against us – we also didn't have the technical equipment we needed. At that point we realised how lacking in experience for this type of ascent we actually were – while we might have done a few climbs, we were by no means hardened mountaineers. That in itself wouldn't have been so much of a problem had we been on a familiar route. But we weren't. Neither of us knew it. It might have been OK if we'd had a mountain guide with us who'd romped up and down the mountain a million times and could have reassured us about the difficulties higher up the ridge. But we didn't. It was just me, Nims and our giant, although now slightly punctured, egos.

We'd no clear idea of what lay ahead of us. It might have been easier than what had just come before. More likely, it would have been much harder. And, on a very practical level, we had a flight to catch the following evening – neither of us had much interest in getting trapped up here. I didn't fancy my death becoming just another footnote in the mountain's history. We looked at each other. It was obvious that we'd both reached exactly the same conclusion: 'We're not doing this.'

People think I'm reckless and blasé in the way I make decisions. They couldn't be more wrong. I'm very calculated. I know where my capabilities lie, and I know when it's time to call it a day. I didn't need to be told I was way out of my depth. So there was no doubt at all, no emotion, no self-recrimination about quitting too easily, or wondering if it was worth waiting to see if the wind would subside. We knew instantly that we'd not be summiting that mountain.

All of this meant that on the plane on the way back we weren't sitting there wrapped in gloom. Quite the opposite. I eased back into my seat, beer in hand, and thought with satisfaction about the experience I'd gained. I knew that the day would come when I'd return to the Matterhorn, and that when I did, I'd know exactly what it would take to get up to that ridge again. As I saw it, that 'failed' attempt was anything but a waste of time.

I don't fixate on the destination. I don't do it for the glory of the summit. I do it for the sense of adventure and for the lessons I know I'll learn. Getting up as far as we had, with the conditions as they were: that was a victory. I didn't see the fact that we'd not reached the summit as a failure, nor did I think it made us failures. There was no shame in it. The events of those two intense days had taught me more about mountaineering than any book ever could have. I knew I'd be able to make teachers out of the mistakes I'd made. Just as importantly, I felt as if I'd explored the outer edges of my abilities: the only way you can recognise your limitations is if you've tripped over them and fallen flat on your face.

I was reaping the rewards of our attempt on the Matterhorn for months to come. The experience I gained then became an important link in the chain that led to me reaching the top of Mount Everest. Without everything I'd learned and seen on the Matterhorn, on Mount Elbrus in southern Russia (where we'd had to stop 200 metres from the summit) and in Argentina while climbing Aconcagua (where we'd got up to Camp 4 before our attempt had to be abandoned because the winds were too high), I'd never have been able to climb the world's highest mountain.

One way of looking at it was that I prepared for my assault on Everest by failing to summit three other peaks. I could have been demoralised, I could have had a voice in my head going, 'If you couldn't get to the top of a 6,960-metre mountain, how do you think you're going to manage an 8,848-metre one?' Instead I looked at the positives: I'd made it to Camp 4 of Aconcagua. I'd gone part way up the

Matterhorn in the hardest possible conditions. More than that, my experiences on the Matterhorn impressed upon me the importance of understanding the mountain and taking heed of the warnings it gives you. In the beginning we'd ignored them, or perhaps had too little experience to recognise them. I wouldn't allow myself to fall into the same trap twice.

And having been in the middle of a storm up the Matterhorn prepared me for a similar experience on Everest. I knew I could be in that position where visibility was reduced almost to zero, my face lashed by wind and snow, and that I could hold my nerve.

THOSE BANKABLE MOMENTS

We've all got a flame inside us. It's the thing that drives and inspires us, it's what keeps us excited and gives us purpose in life. When my flame starts to flicker, I've got to go out and open new spaces in which I can learn and grow and become a better version of myself. I can't let it go out, so I have to keep it lit. If I'm comfortable being comfortable, then I feel like I'm on autopilot.

I feel sorry for those people living in the grey, mundane void who never experience any emotion beyond mild contentment or mild discomfort. And I pity those who are too busy living in the past or trying to predict the future to realise that if you tackle life head on, you'll reap the most amazing rewards. I don't want to be on my death bed saying, 'I wish I had my time again.' That's why I tried to climb the Matterhorn in winter. I wanted to expose that fear, I wanted to feel those emotions again, I wanted to peel yet more layers off.

I was prepared to fail because I knew that the positive benefits of just *attempting* it would outweigh anything I could achieve by sitting safely at home. In fact, everything I've done in my life has been a matter of trial and error. There have been as many failures as there have been successes. When something goes wrong I just re-attack the situation, and nine times out of ten I fall flat on my face. But then I pick myself up, dust myself off and crack on. No experience is wasted.

It's through this process of pushing myself and making mistakes that I've learned so much about what I can and can't do, and it's a crucial part of the positive mindset I've developed over time. Lots of people are so frightened of failing that it becomes a huge obstacle that stops them from becoming the best possible versions of themselves. I can't even begin to tell you how frustrating I find this.

If I hear one more person say, 'Oh, I didn't know I was capable of that,' I'll rip their heads off. On my day camps I'll have people in front of me holding sandbags above their heads. They'll be straining, faces red, veins bulging, and with what breath they've got left they'll be saying, 'I can't hold it any longer,' at the very same time as I'm telling them that they can. And they always can. They didn't think they could do it, and it was only me shouting at them that showed them that it was indeed possible. What they need to do is to develop their own voice telling them that they can do more.

People get overly focused on the destination. I want them to pay more attention to the journey. It's like what I say about being afraid of heights. If you've taken two footsteps closer to the edge of that cliff, but then ultimately you didn't abseil down it like you'd planned, then you're still further on than you've ever been. It's still a victory. You've opened up new space for yourself. Next time you'll probably get even closer. This is what I call 'exposure'. It's so important, and you have to bank it.

These are the bankable moments, the small percentages that accrue day after day, week after week, month after month. Nobody leaps from 0 to a 100 in one bound. Breaking things down into small, achievable bits like this creates a constant sense of momentum. You go through life excited because you're constantly pushing your boundaries, expanding your sense of what you thought was possible. Eventually, you get to that point where, although you may not be invincible, nothing fazes you.

That, for me, is one of the keys to life.

BE AN EXTREME DOER

I think sometimes I go too far in identifying with others. I really have to make a concerted effort to step *out* of their shoes. Because I understand them, I find myself wanting to take them on my path, but I know I can't – my path isn't necessarily the right one for them. Submerging yourself like that in somebody else's personality isn't good for you either. There are times when all I want to do is just take away all of their problems, as if by magic.

That's when I catch myself. I look at them and think, *You've got to go through this. I can't do it for you.* It might seem like a negative experience – it will probably feel like one – but it's you who needs to come out the other side. If it's just magicked away, what new skills will you have learned? What will you have come to understand about yourself and your capabilities? I can't fix other people. It's their journey, their life. I can point them in a certain direction, pass on what I know, but I can't – and won't – carry them down that road. It would be the worst thing I could do. All I can do is give them a couple of words, a couple of actions, for them to hold on to.

Lived experience in the world is essential. You have to get out there and learn things for yourself, because at the end of the day, only you have the answers. No team leader, no psychologist can tell you if something feels right.

I'm not an intellect. I'm not a bookworm. I'm an extreme doer. Which means that I'm always a bit sceptical when I hear about somebody's academic qualifications, or all the courses they've been on. It's not that I don't think these achievements are impressive in themselves. But theoretical knowledge only takes you part of the way. What I really want to ask them is, have you *experienced* it? Have you worked for it? Have you gone out of your way to expose yourself to those hardships and sufferings in order to really understand it? I could have done all the reading in the world ahead of my attempt on the Matterhorn, but trying, and failing, to reach the summit taught me so much more than any book ever could have.

Theoretical knowledge has its place, and yet it doesn't really compare to those lessons that you can really feel under your skin. Once you've felt it, you'll go, *Fuuuuuck*; you'll be able to connect things together. When your heart and mind are connected, it's one of the most powerful forces in the world. You'll only truly understand something if action and intellect are working hand in hand.

This is true even on the most mundane level. Think about learning to ride a bike when you were a kid. No matter how much time somebody might spend telling you about the physics involved, or explaining the finer points of the technique, you won't ever be able to actually go out there and bomb along the road without stabilisers unless you've tried it for yourself, and, in all likelihood, scraped your knee a few times in the process.

Go out there, make mistakes, find out things about yourself. You won't regret it.

DON'T FIXATE ON A DESTINATION, FOCUS ON THE JOURNEY

A lot of the contestants on *SAS: Who Dares Wins* come on the show wearing a full suit of body armour: it's our job to prise it off one piece at a time and help them become the best version of themselves they can be. *We* don't change their lives; that change really comes from them. They come to us because there's a part of them that already wants to do something different. All we do is hand them the tools; show them what they're really capable of. That's what I love so much about it.

But we deliberately don't tell the contestants anything about what's in store for them. If we gave them the full course outline at the beginning of the ten days, I guarantee they'd be out of there like a bullet. As long as they're willing to enter the commitment phase – that willingness to stay on for this task, and the next, and the next – it'll get to the point where it's *easier* to carry on than it is to turn back. More than that, they'll be doing things that only a week before they had no idea they were capable of.

It was the same with me. When I joined the army as a raw sixteen-year-old, I did so because I wanted to be self-sufficient. I didn't have a grand plan or anything; if you'd told me I would end up in the Special Forces I'd have laughed at you; it wasn't even in my head to go for it. I would have seen it as way beyond anything I was capable of. Instead I focused on the journey, what was immediately in front of me.

I took every challenge on I could, then looked for what was next. First I was best recruit; then best at PT; then I joined P Company of the Paras; then I went from being a Marine to training as a sniper; then putting myself forward for the SBS and becoming a team leader.

What I learned is that you can never go straight from 0 to 100. If something seems too good to be true, it probably is. All that will do is damage you. I couldn't have possibly gone from being a raw recruit to a Tier One Special Forces operator overnight. Had some miracle or oversight meant that I'd been allowed to do so, I'd probably have been dead within seconds of my first mission.

Similarly, if you try to run a marathon from a standing start, without any training, it will leave you so traumatised that you'll never want to put trainers on again. Much better to start off by doing a 5K, then a 10K, then a half-marathon. And then, even if you do end up having to stop at mile sixteen, you can look back and see how far you've come and appreciate the foundations you've laid. Sixteen miles is still further than you've ever run in your life before. It's something to be celebrated. If you've headed out without doing any sort of prep and end up fucked after five miles, then you'll have robbed yourself of that sense of achievement.

THE POSITIVE POWER OF COMMITMENT

The most important thing to me is the moment when you decide to commit to something. Once you're committed, the destination isn't important. Forget it. What's important is that you've stepped into that new space of trying things, learning, getting used to the feeling of pushing yourself. You can stay there for weeks, months, just thinking, 'Wow, this is actually quite exciting to me.'

That's what gives me purpose in life. A lot of people don't commit because they look at the destination and all they can think about is how they're going to fail. But nine times out of ten you'll find that even if things don't go entirely how you want them to, you're left thinking, 'Oh, that wasn't too bad.' And it gives you the confidence to commit again. And again. And again. It may be that you end up taking a different route from the one you first intended, but there comes a point when you realise that what looked like a failure has been flipped into a success.

The funny thing about failure is that it's everywhere. I'm going to fail and fail and fail again until the day I die. When you realise that failure is just an everyday part of life, like breathing, and you embrace it, you'll be so much freer; that'll be the moment that you make it work for you.

Positivity is about committing to failure. Lots of people see failure as a dirty word; they're so petrified of making the wrong decision that they listen to every voice except for the one inside them. What will other people think of me? What if it goes wrong? They fear that if they fail, that they'll become a failure themselves. That's bollocks. Just because a lion lets one gazelle slip through its grasp, that doesn't mean he's stopped being an apex predator. It's an incident, nothing more. The only result is that he becomes hungrier, even more determined to make sure the next tasty gazelle doesn't get away.

If you don't commit, you're never going to learn about yourself. It doesn't matter if you don't get to where you were planning to go; what's important is building up all of those small, bankable moments of exposure. Next time a similar opportunity comes along, guess what? You won't be starting from the beginning anymore. All those bankable moments mean you're already halfway there.

GIVE YOURSELF TIME

Very few people really know what they want from life at an early age. If you do have that sort of certainty, then congratulations, you're extremely lucky. The rest of us have got to spend a big chunk of time working it out.

The good news is that you've got time on your side, as people are maturing later and later. For most, life doesn't even really start until they leave college or university, and by that point they're into their twenties. When I think about myself when I was twenty-one … I didn't have a clue.

At that age you still have your whole life ahead of you. It's the perfect time for trying things out. Failing, succeeding, learning: trial and error. That's how you find out who you are and what you connect to. Don't expect to find out what you really want, who you really are, until your thirties, maybe even your forties, possibly even later that.

Look at me. It's only now, as I approach forty, having tried out two or three really different careers, that I've finally found my calling. And even then, I've only got a rough idea of where I want to end up. Do I know exactly how I'll get there? No. But does the path feel right for me, and am I happy and positive? Yes, absolutely.

GO LOOKING FOR TROUBLE

Sometimes I look at challenges and I really don't want to take them on – they look too hard, or the thought of them makes me uncomfortable. Then I think about the possibility of a positive outcome, and something changes. I don't mean material success, I mean personal development; the chance to forge my personality in a new, exciting fashion. That's the way I saw the idea of climbing Mount Everest. It wasn't because I thought I could persuade someone to pay me money and make a TV show, it was because I thought to myself, 'Right, that's a fucking *challenging* situation up there; let's see if we can flip it.' The negative almost won, but I came out the other side.

It's happened to me again and again and again, especially as I've been making steps into the media world. When I started out with *SAS: Who Dares Wins*, for most of the time I didn't really notice the cameras. They followed me about, but they were only ever on the edge of my vision, so after a while I stopped even noticing they were there. Then the producers started to ask me to do pieces to camera. They'd say, 'Right, Ant, look down the camera,' and I'd be like, 'What do they mean, look down the camera? I can't just fucking talk to a camera.'

I remember sitting down for the first time to do a master interview – the bits when I'm talking right down the lens –

and seeing a mirror on the front of the camera, which projected off to someone who was behind the camera and asking the questions. I felt really weirded out by it as it made me incredibly self-conscious. It got to the point where I was so uncomfortable that whenever pieces to camera came up I was gripped by dread. Although I knew by this point that I was committed 100 per cent to the show, and that if I wanted a career on TV this was the sort of thing I'd have to do all the time, I was beginning to wonder if I could carry on.

When the team said, 'Ant, we're doing a master interview now,' they might as well have been saying, 'Ant, we're going to pull your fingernails out.' In fact, I probably would have preferred it if they'd been torturing me. I fucking hated it.

But the fact that it was something that was pushing me well out of my comfort zone, made me understand that it was a skill that I had to learn. No matter how much you love your career, there will always be negative elements that you can't avoid. If you want to carry on doing that job, you need to find a way of overcoming them. In this case I did it by volunteering for *every* piece to camera that came up. Adverts, endorsements, fanbase stuff. Even now I still get a bit uncomfortable, but it gets better every time. And every time, once I've nailed it, I look back and I remember that it wasn't so bad after all.

If there's something that intimidates or unsettles you, throw yourself at it. The more you engage with it, the more you'll strip it of its fearful attributes. What once had been a negative in your life will instead become a positive, one that might open up new avenues.

I know that a point will come when the thought of doing a piece to camera won't trouble me at all – and that's exactly when I'll need to move on and do something else that gets under my skin in the same way. Like acting. I'd love to be an actor. And although I know I'm not ready yet, I also know that I'm moving in the right direction, precisely because I've been doing stuff that takes me out of my comfort zone. If I'd tried to make it straight after leaving the military, the chances are that I wouldn't have got anywhere. But over the last few years I've made so many positive steps, creating all this new space for myself. I know it's a possibility.

BE A PROBLEM SOLVER

I remember when I was training as a sniper, there was another guy who just blew my mind. He was an incredible shot, a natural, but that wasn't enough for him. He was also ferociously dedicated to self-improvement. He carried a little notebook – his sniper log – with him everywhere he went. When we were on the range, practising, he'd mark down the wind speed, the humidity, the barometric pressure and the air pressure in his log, then note the adjustments he'd make to his weapon in order to account for it all and get the perfect shot. He knew that the best way to learn the craft of sniping was to make a record of the conditions in your environment, then just get behind that weapon and shoot round after round after round after round.

Slowly, through a process of sheer repetition, it starts to become instinctive. You begin making your own calculations subconsciously. You find yourself thinking, almost automatically, 'Right, we're 500 metres away, these are the conditions. That means four clicks to the right, two clicks up.'

The secret to his trade was utter meticulousness, making sure no corners whatsoever were cut. The number of variables he had to process was incredible – he needed to know exactly how to breathe; if the shot was further than two kilometres, he had to account for the rotation of the earth – and he had to understand them all, both individually and in concert with each other.

He saw life as a series of problems to be solved and made it his business to find out how. I've tried to take that approach on. The human being is a problem-solving animal. It's one of the factors that underpinned our evolution. Look at history – look at building the first steam engines, producing vaccines for tuberculosis or sending men to the moon. Every single one of us is a problem-solver. But so much of life today is engineered to make things easier and safer for us, and in the process we've become less and less adept at solving problems. It's like a muscle that's wasted away.

I don't want to live my life on autopilot. I want my mind to be racing. That's what I love about life, figuring it out on a daily basis. And for me, solving problems offers a way of training my mind. I get excited when I'm presented with a problem. It's how you find out more about yourself. You can learn about your strengths and weaknesses. Right, I can do this. OK, I can't do that. You might have twenty problems in a day and only find eight answers. Fine, work on those answers. When you know what your limitations are, you can challenge them. It's like hitting a golf ball. The more you hit it, the more you know about the ball, your club, your swing. Something eventually just clicks into place.

Test yourself. Give yourself as many chances to pick up new skills and learn new things about yourself as you can. If you're driving along in your car and you get a puncture, you could call the AA and wait for them to come to fix the tyre for you or you could try to make the repair yourself. Sure, it might take an hour, your hands might end up covered in black grease and you'll probably have sworn your bollocks off. But after you've realised you can do it, you'll feel like a million dollars. Not only that, but you'll have a whole load of confidence that you can take into the next tricky situation you find yourself in. How much better is that than just sitting there helplessly on the hard shoulder waiting to be rescued?

If I'm on a train and when we pull into a station there's an announcement that 'We are delayed here for two hours,'

I'll jump off and find a bus, take a taxi. It might cost a bit more, but I'm keeping that muscle going. I don't want to be like most people and let out a sigh before sitting there like a plum for 120 minutes. It may not be your fault, but it's become your problem. It's up to you whether you take ownership of the situation and try to do something about it.

Challenge everything you do. If you do something well, ask yourself why. If you make a mess of things, pick apart what went wrong and learn from it. The more you get into the habit of solving these small problems, the more likely it is that when you're confronted by a big crisis, your muscle memory will kick in and you'll be better equipped to face up to it. It will be scary at times, but your confidence will grow. You'll store it up, like money in the bank. And, like with so many other aspects of living a positive life, the more you put in, the more you'll get out.

CLEAN YOUR TEETH

Everything starts with you, and it begins with the smallest things. Big, life-changing pieces of good news are few and far between, so it's important to act to maintain your positivity. You don't have to climb Everest or pass selection or ace your exams every day to be making progress towards becoming the best possible version of you. For some people, exposure might simply be a question of stepping outside their front door.

Look after yourself. Make an effort to be kind to yourself. Get up, have a shower, clean your teeth, put on fresh clothes. These things will make you feel better. All of a sudden you won't want to bum around the house anymore; you'll be desperate to go out there, do things. Nobody ever found a job down the back of their sofa.

If you start your day off with a positive act, no matter how tiny, you'll want to follow it with another, because it feels so *good*. Every positive has a knock-on effect. That, ultimately, is the slow-burn pleasure of positivity: the knowledge that every tiny thing you have done has contributed to building something that's greater than the sum of its parts. Nobody has given it to you – you've worked for it.

Think how much nicer and more rewarding a meal that you've cooked for yourself is than something you've ripped the packaging off and bunged into the microwave. Nobody ever got a sense of achievement from reheating a lasagne for two minutes.

When you get into that negative cycle of thinking to yourself 'I don't deserve this,' you're not going to treat yourself well. And what I've learned over the years is that if you're tired, or eating badly, it's far easier to slip into a negative headspace. If you haven't slept properly, your mind will be fogged, and problems that normally you'd be able to bat away assume outsize proportions. I talk a lot about the power of the mind, but to build your mind up you need to provide it with solid physical foundations. Looking after yourself isn't an indulgence, it's a necessity.

It's also important that you keep an eye on your state of mind. I'm not bothered if I have a bad day. Everyone has bad days sometimes. But if you find yourself in a negative mindset, where you're down on yourself and others around you, you need to snap out of it. Because a day will roll into a week, a week will roll into a month and a month will roll into a year. Almost without realising it, you'll have sunk into a permanent slump.

That's the moment to start the process again: get up, have a shower, clean your teeth, put on fresh clothes, and get out and attack the day.

Emilie

It's odd somehow saying this, but I feel very protective of Anthony. More than you'd believe. He'll admit that sometimes I can see danger where he can't. I've got a better antennae for those people who are disingenuous or are looking to exploit him in some way. I've been that way since we first met, but him becoming famous has made me even more cautious.

Anthony wants to help everybody and it's me who has to tell him: 'You can't just say yes to everything and everyone. You have to put yourself first. You can't help them all, you just can't do it.' It's the same impulsive, heart-on-sleeve approach to life that sometimes gets him into trouble. As I said, he does *usually* listen to me when I get that feeling that tells me it's time to be careful. But there are times when he's absolutely determined to go his own way.

For instance, I knew that Anthony's post on Instagram about the coronavirus was a bad idea and told him so. 'What are you doing? You're completely going against what everyone else is saying.'

He hated that, and really snapped at me. 'It's *my* Instagram, I can post what I want.'

'Yes, I know, but you've got to remember how big your audience is. It's not like me with my 200 followers. Nobody cares what I think. And it's such a controversial topic, no matter how well meaning your post is, it's going to get twisted. It's not the right time.'

He didn't listen.

Inevitably, it got misconstrued, because those sorts of things always do. Especially since the government guidelines changed after he'd put it up. It was a heartfelt post, it came from the right place, but people aren't interested in that. I think maybe he occasionally forgets that he is who he is; that he's got a big profile and has to be so much more careful than most people. He's so trusting about the world, he doesn't remember that there are men and women out there who just want to tear him down. I don't want to see Anthony go through that.

What made me so happy was that Anthony was quick to realise the mistake he'd made, and admit to it publicly. That's the example we both want to set to our children. And that's why we both have always seen Anthony's time in prison as a good opportunity to teach our kids a lesson. I can tell them that good people sometimes do bad things. Your dad is an amazing person, but what he did was wrong and he had to be punished for it. There's no way Oakley, for example, would ever fall into the trap of thinking it's somehow cool to go to prison. We've had the chance to show him how much Anthony regrets that misjudgement.

Anthony is much less interested in punishing our children for something they might have done wrong than in getting them to acknowledge what they've done, own their mistake and promise not to do it again. Then he moves on.

LESSONS

Small things make a big difference. Small steps add up to a big leap. Don't make the mistake of thinking you can race from a standing start to top speed in one bound.

Until you're willing to enter that commitment phase, you'll never get anywhere. Be brave and remember that people who never make mistakes never make anything. Learn to see failure as an engine of positive growth.

Never forget that we're a problem-solving animal. Don't let that muscle wither away. Work it, and you'll reap amazing rewards.

Very few people know what, or even who, they want to be until later on in life. You'll only work this out through trial and error. Get out there, try things, make mistakes, and then challenge everything you do.

Examine your successes and failures with the same energy. No experience is wasted if you tackle every situation with a positive mindset.

CHAPTER 8

BE A SHEPHERD NOT A SHEEP

I NEED TO get off the mountain. I need to get off the mountain. I could feel my feet and fingers beginning to tingle with frostbite. Minutes ago I'd experienced the exhilarating feeling of talking to my wife from the highest point on earth – the summit of Mount Everest. Now I knew I was in deep trouble. The wind was blasting at over forty miles per hour. The snow that whipped around my head had reduced visibility to almost zero.

But there was only one way off the mountain, and I was at the back of that queue. There were fifteen climbers ahead of me, each taking seven or so minutes to negotiate this part of the ridge. The maths was against me. I knew I'd be stuck here for a couple of hours, maybe more. I felt like a kid again. I couldn't remember the last time I was so helpless, so vulnerable to my environment. I was convinced that I was going to freeze to death. The guy in front of me had slipped and crashed his head, and was now hanging upside down a metre off the face of the mountain, pinned to a rock with the depthless void yawning beneath him. At first he wasn't moving; then I could see that he was slipping in and out of consciousness. Sherpas had made five, six attempts to rescue him. All had ended in failure. It got to the point where it looked as if they were going to have to cut the rope with a knife, cut him off the mountain. I didn't want to see that, but it was clear that several people, including me, would die if they didn't.

Look away, I remember thinking, don't be a witness to his gruesome fate. But I couldn't help myself. The whole situation has stayed with me with photographic clarity and I can recall every detail of that scene. Time passed brutally slowly, as if it was reluctant to move forward. I'd been standing, locked in my thoughts for two hours. At times it felt as if I wasn't even really there anymore – my body and mind seemed no longer to be connected. The snow had destroyed any frame of reference I might once have had. For most of the time there was no near or far, no up or down. Just white.

Every couple of minutes the whiteout would subside and I'd be able to see maybe twenty metres in front of me. In one of these gaps I saw two more climbers trapped on the ridge. One was screaming and crying. The other was trying to work his way up with his ice axe. I looked slowly from the man beneath me, hanging over the void, to the two in similarly perilous positions a bit further away. Suddenly I became convinced that I wouldn't be getting off the mountain. You'll die here, I thought. For the first time in my life I told myself, Ant, you're dead. I'd never had that feeling before. Even in the worst situations I'd found myself in when I was in the SBS, when missions went wrong, men were hit, I knew that there was always something I could do to affect the situation. Here, everything appeared to be completely out of my control. Now that I was in this position, I could understand why so many people remain frozen up here in the death zone. In those moments I was so fucking close to doing the same.

I was engulfed by an overwhelming sense of panic. The thought that I was going to die had such an unanswerable, inevitable logic that for a handful of seconds I even started to consider unclipping myself from the fixed rope and simply hurling myself off the mountain. The void was there, at my feet. At that moment, this did not feel like an extreme response. It seemed to me to be the *only* response. The voice in my head was insistent. Just jump off the mountain. I didn't want to freeze and be left as a monument to my own pride and ambition. Just jump off the mountain. Ten seconds went by. Outside my body, the wind whistled viciously around my head; inside, there was nothing. I couldn't even feel my heart beating. I was numb.

It was while this thought – *You're dead, Ant* – pulsated in my head that I looked down at my toes. I could still move them! That changed everything. The situation had been telling me that I was dead. My toes flicking up and down inside my boots told a different story. I was still alive. The flame reignited inside me. A new thought took possession of my mind: *You keep going, boy, until you don't know about it anymore. You keep going until you are dead.* That's when adrenaline began to surge through every part of me. Now I was excited, filled with a new urgency, convinced once again that I still had control over my fate.

DIG DEEP

Imagine you're sitting at the bottom of a big dead tree. The branches that spread out above you are blackened and lifeless. You look up and see nothing that makes you think of spring, or energy. But that tree wouldn't still be standing unless there was some life left in it.

If you look hard enough, if you clamber up its trunk and really try, you'll find a couple of green shoots still growing. Then, all you need to do is snap one of these bits of life off, plant it in front of you and concentrate on growing it. There's nothing unrealistic about that perspective – after all, you've already acknowledged that the rest of the tree is dead.

That's what I do when confronted by any negative situation: I look for any positive, however small, however difficult to find. Even though the little budding twig is tiny in comparison to the hulking tree I've taken it from, it gives me something to focus on. You don't need to think about all of the dead branches anymore; they're irrelevant.

Lots of people are unwilling to invest the time and effort needed to challenge negativity. They forget that you cannot have positivity without negativity. There's a difference between being happy and being positive. Being positive involves challenging negativity. People who claim to be blissfully happy sometimes don't even acknowledge that negativity exists. You get a positive mindset by challenging your life, challenging yourself. The paradox is that you can be a positive thinker without being happy.

If you search hard enough, in any situation, you'll always find positivity. That's what I did on Everest. I found that piece of positivity and then built on it. That one spark of positivity burned all of the negativity away. I almost fell victim to letting the magnitude of a situation define me. Instead, I decided to fight on. Not a single thing had changed about the situation, except for my mindset. It was another example of the phenomenal power of positivity.

Ever since that day in France when I realised that although I couldn't do much to change the uncomfortable circumstances I'd been thrown into, I could control how I responded to them, I've always tried to make sure that I'm the one defining the situation rather than have the situation defining me.

This approach was invaluable to me in the Special Forces, when we had space and time to choose our moment. You'd wait in the silence for five minutes, maybe more, listening for any sound or sign that you might be being watched. By the time you got up, ready to begin the walk to target, your ears had become highly attuned to the environment. Every movement of your arms and legs seemed madly amplified – you could hear the crunch of each individual stone under your boots, tightening a strap sounded like the roar of an armoured vehicle. There was an amazing power in those moments. We knew that we had the element of surprise, with the enemy exactly where we wanted them.

But the majority of the time we arrived right on top of the enemy, and were greeted by a hail of gunfire. My first experience of landing on a target was during the day. One moment we were in the helicopter, able to see every detail of our prey with almost terrifying clarity: the RPGs and machine guns pointing menacingly out of its back; the jutting beards of the men in the front seats; even the dents and scratches on its bonnet. The next we were out on the ground, plunging into the hot chaos of the dust cloud. I can remember just thinking: *What do I do? Do I shoot? I can't see anything. I can't tell if anybody's shooting because there's too much noise. What do I do?* All I *could* do was hold my nerve, hold my nerve. Then I came out the other side. *Oh, I can see now.* Those first few seconds, though. Only experience can help you get used to them. There's no training in the world that can replicate that mix of terror and excitement.

I only realised afterwards that how I responded to the hyper-violence and danger of the life I'd chosen was up to me. I could have let the situation define me; started shouting because there were bullets spitting past my shoulder and an overdose of adrenaline coursing through every part of my body. Or I could remain calm, in control. Process every sound, every movement. Keep every angle covered. Never let myself get lost in the chaos of it all. The more in control of myself I was, the more in control of my environment I could be.

When you're in a shitty situation, it's far better to be a shepherd than a sheep. Far better to be able to exert some measure of control, or to be able to make even a small positive step in the right direction, than to be a bleating sheep waiting aimlessly for fate to take its course.

HARD TIMES DON'T LAST FOREVER

The mind is the most important tool that we possess. But when you chip away at everything that surrounds it, and leave people exposed with just their minds for company, a lot of people don't know how to cope. Because they can't see the mind, they neglect to train it. They think it's just the empty space in their head that keeps their ears apart. When people who haven't trained their minds to think positively find themselves under pressure, their brain, which should be the thing that gets them out of that crisis, only serves to make things worse.

I can see how this might happen. It's so easy in stressful situations, especially those over which we have little control, to feel completely overwhelmed – they can have a paralysing effect. That's exactly what happened to me on the summit of Everest. I wasn't just flooded with negativity; I was convinced there was nothing I could do. I was in a slump so deep I barely recognised myself.

It was only by thinking positively that I dragged myself off that mountain. It was another reminder to me that you cannot tackle a negative situation with a negative mindset. What saved me was realising that I couldn't let that negative situation dictate to me how I should feel. I couldn't stop the snow or the wind, or speed up the queue, but I could control my response to all of these things. The moment I told myself I was alive, I knew that I was back in charge of the situation.

When I find myself in positions that could inspire negativity, I try to challenge everything. I begin by reminding myself that every situation is different. Different mountain, different people around you, different weather conditions. There is no turn-key solution that will help everyone, no matter what the conditions. Then I break what I'm facing down so that I don't get overwhelmed. Pick it apart. No matter what's going on around me, I'll interrogate myself. 'What am I feeling?' Fear. 'OK, what does that mean?' It's my body getting ready for that step into the unknown. When you do that, what seemed like a relentless assault will be something you can understand. When you can understand it, you can process it. And when you've processed something, you can control your response to it.

Then, if you can identify that an emotion, like fear or sadness or anger, is working against you, you're able to turn it round. When I was feeling broken by my father's death and I slept on his grave, I turned that big wave of emotion into a positive by joining the Marines. I gave my existence purpose, put myself in a position where, once again, I felt part of something.

It's positivity that enables you to take the initiative. Once you begin to exert control, even if to begin with it's only over tiny elements, you'll be moving in the right direction, building momentum. For me, activity is like an engine for generating positivity. On Everest, it was the moment when I wriggled my toes and began to move that everything changed. It was the smallest thing, and it didn't change the fact that the snow was still swirling around my head, the wind was as vicious as it had been seconds earlier and my way out of the situation was going to be arduous. But it completely altered the dynamic. Once you've located that tiny speck of hope, you can build and build and build with it.

Emotional resilience is what will help you withstand any situation. And, just like the human muscular system, it's something that can be built up over time. I've built my emotional resilience up by exposing it constantly to adversity, and tripping over again and again and again. I started doing this after we moved to France after my father's death, and I continued to do the same when spending most of my adult life in some of the most dangerous places on the planet. If I'd suddenly broken down and started weeping while I was kicking down doors in Afghanistan then, guess what, my pals would have been dead. I'd be dead. There were times when I wanted to run away. But I knew I couldn't. Instead I told myself to get a grip, suck it up, and go in there and do the job. I would let my emotions out, but only when I got back off the target.

Learning when to give our emotions free rein and when to control them is such an important life skill, and a crucial part of maintaining a positive mindset. Whether you're angry, sad, upset, suffering or scared, you should be able to control these emotions within yourself, not let them overpower you.

This is why I'm not always sympathetic when I hear people saying things like, 'Kids should be able to express their emotions whenever they want.'

It sounds great, but then I always ask them, 'Is anger an emotion?'

'Yes.'

'So, whenever they feel angry, should they just go around and beat people up, or break things? Is that acceptable?'

'Well, no.'

It's the same with the idea that men should be comfortable crying in public. Yes, of course, we all need a release valve. But all the time? In a meeting? Would that be appropriate?

MAKE NEGATIVITY YOUR FUEL

Once you've reached the point where you can identify and process what you're feeling, you'll also be able to start flipping that negative energy into positive outcomes. I can't even begin to explain to you what a powerful tool that is to have. At its simplest, you might use aggression and violence to win a boxing match. But there are myriad applications.

However, negative thoughts and negative energy can only be used if the motivator is positive. If you don't have a positive outcome in mind, then you'll just be driven off the road by all of these out-of-control emotions. It's like pissing into the wind.

What happens, if, for instance, you're in your car and another driver cuts you up? You start shouting at him. He pulls over, you have a fight. You might experience aggression and anger, but what can you actually achieve? What is the positive outcome? *You* won't be using those negative emotions. *They'll* be using you. Whereas when I used anger to get off the top of Everest, I was doing so to keep alive. It's the same when it comes to my response to other people having a go at me. I love their criticism because it makes me want to work harder, earn more money, buy another house, take my kids on another holiday.

People watching me on *SAS: Who Dares Wins* think they see me ripping people apart. But what I'm always aiming for is personal development. I want that person whose face I'm getting into to become the best version of themselves that they can possibly be. I'm using negative characteristics such as anger and aggression to achieve a positive outcome.

It's the same thing Michael Jordan did when he played for the Chicago Bulls. His relentless commitment to excellence meant that he never let up on his teammates for a second. He was always demanding more from them, to the point where some of them didn't like him, and others were actually afraid of him. He fucking *fought* with them. But every single player, when they looked back on those years of unbelievable success they enjoyed, knew that it wouldn't have been possible if, instead of seizing on their every mistake and pushing them harder than they thought necessary at the time, Jordan had just chased popularity.

In the second celebrity series of *SAS: Who Dares Wins* I had a run-in with Tony Bellew, the cruiserweight world champion. He suffered massively from anger issues, partly because he'd retired the previous year, and partly because he was an aggressive person anyway. For a long time he'd been able to vent all of his rage by training and boxing, and then when he stepped away from the ring he lost not only this outlet, but also a sense of purpose and belonging. I could see this, because exactly the same thing had happened to me when I left the military.

I reckon I'm pretty good now at telling quickly whether somebody is likely to be a positive or negative person. You look at the way they're sitting or their eye movement. Give me a few seconds and I'll know whether they're nervous, frightened, have an attitude or are trying to hide something. Why? Because I've been there. I've been that scared young boy struggling with a great loss, I've been that violent adult. I've tried to hide things and found that they only hurt me when I did so. I know how these emotions work.

Everything about Tony screamed this. The way he talked, the way he clenched his fists, the way he looked at me. And because I'd identified these things in him straight away, I began by putting more and more and more pressure on him. I wanted him to flip out. Every time he couldn't do something, he'd lose it with himself, and end up shouting 'Fuck's sake' and punching the ground. He was also the first guy we brought into the Mirror Room. As soon as we whipped his hood off, I told him he was a danger to himself. That he was a ticking time bomb.

But he was still in denial and wasn't having it at all. I said to him that the only reason I was saying this was because I'd been there myself. I was riling him up again before we sent him back to sleep on it. I knew he'd either wake up and acknowledge that he needed to sort himself out, or he'd be even more angry. He woke up *raging*. And I thought to myself: perfect.

I carried on turning the screw. It got to the point where the producers took me to one side and said, 'Be careful, he's a big boy, he's liable to turn round and lamp you.' He was looming over me, clenching his fists and I was shouting back, 'Come on, this is the time and place, do it! Do it!' He'd never been challenged like that before, not outside the ring anyway. The screw was being turned tighter, tighter, tighter. I could see he was about to just fucking *go*.

And then he got it. I could see the moment when everything changed for him. Just looking at his eyes and the way that his anger almost fled his body, it was clear that he now realised that I was there for him. I wasn't trying to push him for the sake of it, but because I wanted to get through to him. From that moment on he was a different man. He knew that he was in charge of his demons, not the other way around. Amazing.

At the end of the show, Tony texted me to say that I'd done more for him in those eight days than anybody had in his whole life. I can see how my actions towards him – getting into his face, trying to provoke him – could be seen as negative by some people. 'Look at that toxic masculinity; look at this brain-dead barbarian.' No, that's personal sacrifice. I was willing to put myself in harm's way for his personal development. You can't get any more powerful than personal sacrifice. That's what we did in war. We were willing to give everything for our pals and Queen and Country.

It was a good example of the way you can use a negative emotion – aggression – for positive purposes: Tony's personal development. And it worked because my motivator was positive. I was willing to make a sacrifice to achieve a positive outcome.

That's something people sometimes miss about positivity. They think it's just about smiling all the time. Actually, no, it's hard work, and I'd never try to hide that. Most people don't want to suffer; they're unwilling to go through hardship or risk, even when the end goal is worth the effort.

Being positive is not about taking the easy option.

LIVE IN THE PRESENT TENSE

My early experience of loss and dislocation taught me one very valuable lesson: life can change with the flick of a switch. One minute you're standing there, the next minute you're not. One minute this person is part of your life, the next they've been hit by a fucking bus.

I could have gone two ways with that knowledge. It could have made me overly cautious, the sort of person who's always trying to second-guess the future. Instead, I decided that this sort of obsessive, catastrophic thinking is a waste of time. People lose years of their lives worrying about things that *could* happen. And in doing so, huge chunks of their life – opportunities, experiences, people – will completely pass them by. I work on the basis that things won't go wrong, but if they do, fine, I'll react to it. That's life. Shit happens, get on with it. I take each lesson, each experience, as it comes.

By the same token, I understood from a very young age that no matter how much you might want to, you can't change the past. Something has happened, it's gone. That would've, should've, could've world doesn't exist. It's not real.

OWN YOUR HISTORY

I talked in *The Fear Bubble* about how, in the grim days after my arrest, someone in my defence team told me that if I claimed I had PTSD, I'd be able to avoid prison. I know now with absolute conviction that had I gone down the route of feigning PTSD, and attended the courses telling me how much of a victim I was, I'd not be here today. That label – the guy with anger issues who was the 'victim' of war and a troubled childhood – would have come to define me. I would be living a lie, and I wouldn't be doing TV work, or writing books, or any of the amazing opportunities that have opened up to me in the years since.

We've all done things in our past that we regret or are ashamed of. That's just part of life. You might have made a mistake. Who hasn't? But that's only 1 or 2 per cent of who you are. You can't let that minuscule percentage engulf the rest of your identity. People will want to bring you down. They'll dredge up your past and you might have a horrible sense that they know you. After I left prison, I struggled to get a job for a while. The attitude I encountered was: we can't employ him, he's been behind bars. They saw the fourteen-month sentence and felt they were in a position to form a judgement. But they didn't know the other 98 per cent of me. They didn't know the loving, compassionate, family-oriented man, the driven worker, the guy who's willing to make sacrifices to take care of the people he loves most. As I said in *The Fear Bubble*, as long as you're brutally honest with yourself, there's nothing that other people can say that you won't know already. You can just bat that back. Thanks very much, dickhead. It frees you to be yourself and stops anybody from defining who you are.

There are some people, however, who go to prison, and that's them done. They define themselves as a criminal and they let others define them as a criminal, and without really thinking about it they've shut themselves off from huge chunks of life. It's like Mike Tyson says when he's interviewed: people perceive me as an animal? Fine, I'll behave like an animal. This guy was one of the most talented, charismatic boxers of all time, and yet he let others define him and behaved accordingly.

I never wanted to be restricted in that way, and I don't think others should. I think sometimes people use genuine if perhaps minor reasons for not doing something as a way of avoiding confronting deeper reasons that they don't want to consciously acknowledge.

When I was doing all the admin ahead of signing up for the first series of *SAS: Who Dares Wins*, somebody handed me a DBS (Disclosure and Barring Service) form and told me to fill it in. I decided I'd ignore it. If I'd completed it, they'd have seen I'd been to prison, made a lot of assumptions, and that would have been game over. It wasn't a lie; it was an omission. I just didn't tell them.

Nobody mentioned it again, and I didn't give it a second thought. The first episode pulled in big numbers and it was clear that we were about to be part of something potentially very exciting. That's when I got a call from Minnow Films, the production company behind the show. I was standing outside BBC Radio Chelmsford, about to go in for an interview, when my phone rang.

'Ant, is this rumour true?'

I had no fucking idea what they were talking about. 'What rumour?'

'That you've been to prison.'

'Yeah, yeah, it's true. Who's interested in that? Who would give a shit?'

They were really pissed off, asking why they hadn't known about it before. So I explained that I hadn't lied, and that I'd wanted them to see me for what I was capable of doing, not for something that, for me at least, lay firmly in my past.

I didn't know about the whole celebrity side of things and didn't realise that almost overnight I'd become somebody that the media were interested in. Then I got hauled in to Channel 4 and we had the whole conversation over again. There were a few sickening moments when I thought, 'Oh shit, it's over before it's really begun.'

And then one of the producers said, 'Look, Ant, we'd have hired you anyway. We just wished you felt you could have been straight with us,' and I said, 'I absolutely appreciate that, but I just didn't want to be defined by my criminal record.' Fair play to them, they embraced the whole thing. They understood that if you don't make mistakes in life, you don't make anything.

When the inevitable story ran, in the *Daily Mirror* a few days later, there were headlines accusing me of being a hypocrite. They said I was out there on the show laying into people, but all the while harbouring a dark secret of my own. Channel 4 valued my work ethic, they knew how determined I was to make the show a success and had made the decision to judge me on my performance, not my past, so they stood by me. I always try to do the same. I judge people at face value. I won't go on their CV, and I'm especially careful not to pay any attention to what others tell me. I'm never going to be negative towards somebody just because I've heard negative things about them. But if you show me that you're negative, I'll probably keep my distance.

By embracing the fact that I'd made a terrible mistake in punching that police officer, and talking about the ways prison changed me, I robbed this part of my past of its power. But for a lot of people, the real struggle isn't just coming clean to the world about aspects of their past; it's admitting it to themselves. If you try to bury events from your past, no matter how hard you try, you'll never succeed in repressing them completely. You're just storing up trouble for later. Those feelings or secrets always find a way of creeping up on you when you least expect it.

So many of the contestants on *SAS: Who Dares Wins* come to us very obviously struggling with an aspect of their past. Some people have been bereaved, or experienced horrific abuse. What I find inspiring about this is that the very fact that they've entered the show indicates that they know they have to confront whatever it is they've been through. That's a first positive step. In the last series there was James, whose family had a reputation as criminals. He never tried to hide this, but at the same time his determination to break free from it shone through. He knew that you can either let your past become a millstone around your neck, or you can use it as fuel to push you on to better things.

DON'T TRY TO KEEP UP
WITH FASHION

There are fashions in behaviour just as much as there are in clothes. And they come and go just as quickly. People will go along with what's out there just so that they're accepted and they can lead easy lives. They'll be so desperate to conform that they'll say things they don't believe, and along the way they'll lose themselves.

Ultimately, that's a negative way of living your life, and another way of letting a situation define you rather than the other way around. Saying things just because you think that's what others want to hear from you is a corrosive habit. Once you start to listen to other people's opinions rather than your own, you'll begin to doubt your own choices and decisions.

This is even more true when it comes to bringing up children. In my opinion, there are a lot of distractions going on in society that just confuse your kids. Children are so much happier when things are kept black and white. I want to be a positive male role model, but doing that isn't the same as saying, 'Yes, go ahead, do whatever you want.' If that means saying things that other people won't agree with or will disapprove of, I can live with that.

I want to be honest with myself, and I want my children to learn to be the same. So I tell my kids to be happy with who they are. I tell my son what his strengths and weaknesses as a man are, and I tell my daughter what her strengths and weaknesses as a woman are. For instance, men are physically stronger than women. If that wasn't true you'd have women fighting men at heavyweight level or UFC, or playing them at rugby. That's why I also make sure that my son knows that men should be looking to protect those weaker than them. That's what we do. If I saw a woman being hit by a man, you better believe I'm going over there. If I see a woman struggling with a suitcase on the Tube or broken down by the side of the road, you better believe I'll stop to see if I can help. And I'd want my son to do the same. 'When I'm not here,' I tell him, 'you need to help Mummy out. You need to be the man of the house. Take the bins out. Help Mummy with the cleaning.'

Most of all, though, I want them to grow up with a stable sense of the world and have the confidence to figure things out for themselves, and know that there's no need to conform to what everyone else is saying. As they get older, my kids might challenge my values. Great. I'll be delighted if they do.

Emilie

SAS: Who Dares Wins turned our family life upside-down. I'd
had a husband whose job was so secret that even I didn't know
where he was a lot of the time. I couldn't tell anybody other than
my family and closest friends what he did. We weren't supposed
to have any sort of social media or anything like that. We used
to share a phone.

Then almost overnight we went from an existence where
nobody knew anything about my husband and how he was
spending his time, to realising that millions of people thought
they knew *everything* about him. I'd meet people on the street
and they'd talk to me about Anthony as if they knew him, and all
I'd be thinking was, 'This is really strange.'

For a year, maybe more, I struggled to adjust to it. I'm a pretty
private person – I don't like anyone knowing my business – and
suddenly there were all these people who were able to see
parts of my life that I'd never shared with anyone close, let
alone strangers. It wasn't me in the limelight, and yet still I was
having to answer questions I'd never been asked before. It was
all really invasive.

When you're married to somebody famous you understand very quickly that the days of you being able to control every element of your life are over. Most people hadn't known about Anthony going to prison, not even our kids. I'd just told them that he was away working in Africa. As far as our children were concerned, everything was normal. Then the papers got hold of it and I was finding myself having to explain a private decision I'd taken years before to my job, and the school. Other people would be able to choose how and when their children learned something big like that. It was taken out of our hands.

We were all caught by surprise by the impact that *SAS: Who Dares Wins* had on us. Before Anthony was approached to become the chief instructor, we were about to move to South Africa. There wasn't any part of us that thought the show would become what it has. We needed the money to help us start our new life, so we thought doing the programme would give us a boost. In our heads it would be a one-off show watched by ten people. Instead it exploded overnight.

Anthony suddenly had this audience of millions. Out of everything, it was this that I found hardest. Partly because it felt as if all these people I didn't know and would never meet were watching us, and partly because Anthony got so wrapped up in it that for a little while I thought we might lose him. He'd be there, in the same room as his family, tapping on his phone, oblivious to us because he was sending messages to this or that fan. He was with us, and yet at the same time he wasn't really *there*.

It went to his head, and stuff teetered a bit for us. That's not a shock. If I had thousands of strangers sending me messages on Instagram telling me how great I was, I bet my head would swell up too. Who wouldn't float up in that bubble? Anyone who says it wouldn't affect them is lying.

I spent a lot of time bringing him back down to earth, mostly by nagging at him. A pretty old-school approach to a very modern problem, but one that worked. After a while he got to a point where he realised that the other world was fickle; it wasn't real life. He saw that desire the media have to build you up and knock you down, and although it was a bit of a hard landing, it did him a lot of good.

I think underneath everything, he'd always known that family and close friends were what really mattered. Everything else, as glitzy and exciting as it might have looked to begin with, was irrelevant. Who cares what strangers think? It's lovely to have people you've never met messaging you to tell you how great you are, but what do they really know? And if you begin to let them define your self-worth, that means that when keyboard warriors decided to have a pop – and they will, they always do – you have to take them seriously too.

LESSONS

You can't always change your environment. You can, however, change the way you perceive it. If you're able to control your emotions, you'll ensure that it's you defining the situation you're in rather than the situation defining you.

Every situation has a positive seed in it. It doesn't matter how negative it might seem at first glance, if you're willing to put the work in, you'll always find the positive.

Doing something, no matter how small, is always better than doing nothing. When you're acting, you're refusing to allow the situation to define you. You've started to define that situation.

Negativity is a fact of life. We all have negative emotions, we all find ourselves in negative situations. But you can learn to harness this negative energy and use it in a positive direction.

Don't let negative elements in your past stop you from having a positive future. Acknowledge the bad things you've done or experienced, but remember they only represent a tiny percentage of who you really are.

Fashions in behaviour and values come and go. Stay true to your own beliefs and don't give in to the pressure to conform.

CHAPTER 9

GIVE THEM ENOUGH ROPE

THE JUNGLE GETS into your head. For some people it's an obsession, for others it's a living nightmare. There's no middle ground. Me, I love it. I love its richness and power. I love that moment as you fly overhead when you can see the humidity rising off the dense green carpet of trees. It looks beautiful, so much so that it can sometimes make you feel as if your heart has grown.

Then, when you're actually in among it, the sheer scale is too much for your brain to process. It excites me and petrifies me at the same time. There's no real way to absorb the brute fact of its enormity. So much of it is unsurveyed, uncharted. It's one of the few places where you can take a handful of steps away from the track and think to yourself: no human being has ever been here before. I always get a flash of what the prehistoric world must have been like. Vast swathes of nothingness that at the same time contain multitudes.

This means that life beneath the canopy is disorienting, claustrophobic. You have to really know what you're doing.

You can walk for five metres, then turn around and realise you can't trace back where you started. Or you can walk from six in the morning until six at night and, if you're lucky, you might cover a couple of miles. Every step will have looked the same, so you have no sense of progress. There's never a moment when you can say with satisfaction, 'Look how far we've come.' You might as well be on a tread-mill. I often think of those conscript kids from Brooklyn or Compton, just dropped into the Vietnamese jungle and told to patrol areas of unforgiving terrain as big as entire coun-tries. No wonder they were high half the time.

And yet there's nobody else around, no police station, no bars, no rules or regulations. There's no terrain on the planet that offers the same freedom as the jungle. It's just you and nature in its purest, most elemental condition: delicate shafts of light arrowing through the canopy, the dink, dink, dink of water dripping off the trees like a metronome.

It comes alive at night. It's pitch black, but if you lie in your hammock and switch your torch on, you can look down and see that the whole floor is moving. Ants, more ants than you ever thought existed. Then, when you wake up in the morning, they're all gone, and you're left wonder-ing whether perhaps the things you saw and heard the night before were just a hallucination.

The silence in the day is as unsettling as the symphony of noise you hear after dark. You realise that you never knew how loud a twig could crack. Over time you learn ways of moving that are more discreet, and which leave as few traces of your existence as possible. This is essential if you're fighting in the jungle, because just being there heightens your senses. Once you're settled into jungle life, after three or four days you can smell a newcomer from metres away. Your nostrils are suddenly assailed by the soap that they use and the detergent in which their clothes have been washed. You might even be able to work out what they last ate.

It's the most challenging environment a soldier can operate in. It can feel like everything wants to bite you, scratch you, sting you, drown you; the canopy wants to swallow you up; the humidity is overwhelming, and leaves you sweating constantly. Every step you take is an exercise in uncertainty because you don't know whether you're going to come across a snake or a strand of vine. I've seen the best soldiers fall short after two or three days. They can't deal with the insects, the heat, the terrain – or the danger.

If you get scratched on a windswept hillside in Scotland, you'll probably be OK. If you do the same in the jungles of Sierra Leone and catch an infection, you might just have handed yourself a death sentence.

And when it rains, it fucking *rains*. Flash floods can clear out the whole area as you sleep, propelled by swollen rivers that explode their banks. The other risk caused by heavy rain is deadfall. Rotten branches balanced precariously in the canopy can be dislodged. Suddenly you look up and what looks like an entire tree is plunging down on top of you. It's the biggest killer in the jungle.

You can't fight the jungle; you have to embrace it. When I was there I quickly understood I couldn't beat it. It had been there for thousands of years; it had its way of living and I knew I had to accommodate myself to it. There's no way of forcing the jungle into a shape that suits you. If you don't like being covered head to toe in mud, you're not going to get on with it. If you flail and struggle against the vines, you'll get nowhere. You have to be patient in a positive way – find its groove and fit into it.

Me, I thought, *Fucking great, no need to put on cam cream. I can use it to my advantage.* There's so much out there that you can live on, whether it's a particular plant you can eat or a vine you can use to help you make things. It'll reward you if you've made the effort to understand it. It will punish you if you haven't. If you can operate in the jungle, you can survive anywhere in the world.

WHEN I WAS told we'd be filming an episode of *Escape* in the jungles of Papua New Guinea I was buzzing. The disaster that we were going to be trying to extricate ourselves from was the aftermath of a flash flood. Then, along with a team of engineers, I was supposed to cobble together a machine from the debris we found that would help us get to safety. They were there to do the clever calculations and technical work; my job was to keep them alive.

We were dropped off in a location miles from the nearest village, surrounded by swamp, mud and crocodiles. A fire engine and a 250cc motorbike lay on the river bed, both with their engines flooded by water. There was a wrecked passenger bus washed up on the north side of the bank, and further up the river was a 4x4 that was missing one of its front wheels.

Somewhere among those mangled machines were the parts and tools we'd need to construct the vehicle that would help us navigate to safety. But for twelve hours of each day they were all submerged beneath the tidal river's deep brown water.

It was horrendous. We only had the clothes we were in and a basic ration of food and water – enough for six days if we were careful. Everything else, such as shelter and sanitation, was entirely up to us. Given that just surviving in the jungle is hard enough, let alone trying to build anything, I knew from the beginning that we were up against it.

A lot depended on how well the contestants worked together as a team. Good teamwork is about everybody within that team being willing to be brutally honest with themselves. It's about being humble enough to step back when your weakness presents itself, and allowing somebody else to show their strength. When a team works like this, it can work ten times as fast and effectively as a dysfunctional unit that's full of competing egos and people who aren't prepared – or able – to admit their weaknesses. Egos waste hours and create tension and stop a team from fulfilling its potential.

My weaknesses were on show for everybody to see. I wasn't an engineer, so I knew that the best thing I could do was step back and stay out of the experts' way. I could find them food and water, and act as a pair of strong arms when they needed a hand, but if I tried to interfere with the intricate work of salvaging and design, I'd be more trouble than help.

I knew that over time the contestants' individual weaknesses would reveal themselves, but I was also aware that in a paradoxical way their biggest strengths as engineers were also their biggest weaknesses. I realised very quickly that I'd be managing individuals with strong opinions and a deep faith in their own abilities. They were all experts in their field, equipped with the intellectual tools they needed to get their particular job done. Each of them was used to being able to control procedures down to the tiniest details, because doing so mattered. Engineers that build bridges have to plan to perfection; in their trade, the smallest mistakes can cost lives and cause devastation.

I'd be out of my comfort zone because you could write what I know about engineering on a very small postage stamp; they'd be out of their comfort zone because instead of a world of blueprints and precision-tooled equipment, they'd be plunged into the chaos of the jungle environment. At some point I knew that I'd have to manage failure, the number one hurdle that stops us from achieving everything we want. I wanted to know how these men and women would respond when things went wrong.

As soon as we got into the jungle I started testing their characters, trying to see what their blind spots were. The first job was to build a camp at the water's edge on a safe part of the river bank. We knew it was going to be a wet, miserable, cold night. We also knew we didn't have that much time to build a shelter and would need everybody to pitch in. We had ten, maybe fifteen minutes of light left. When the jungle gets dark, it does so instantly. One minute you can see, just. The next you won't even be able to make out your hand in front of your face. If we could cling together on a communal bed and keep ourselves off the ground to put a bit of distance between us and all the creepy-crawlies, we stood a chance of staying half-warm and getting some sleep. Most of the rest of the team seemed to agree. One guy did not.

Ed was thirty, an electrical engineer. He had long, straggly hair, like one of the less frightening characters from *Pirates of the Caribbean*, and that pale sort of face you can only get if you spend more time in a darkened room than outside in the fresh air. I wondered when the last time was he'd seen the sun. He'd walked into the jungle with a jaunty swagger, talking about how keen he was to face complex problems, and gave off the distinct impression that *he'd* be the one to solve this jigsaw puzzle. You could call it arrogance.

Positivity is about having an open mindset – being alive to possibility and new ideas. Ed was completely the opposite. He had a very fixed idea about how things should be done and found it really hard to deviate from that. This one-way perspective leads to negative outcomes. Why cut yourself off like that? Other people's ideas might seem way off-field, but why deprive yourself of the chance to pick up a little gem along the way?

'I'm going to lay my cards on the table,' Ed announced in his petulant, slightly nasal voice as we were discussing how to build our home for the next few days. 'I'm going to have my solo shelter here. I'm going to sleep six inches off of the ground without any spiders on me under a pitched roof. I don't want to sleep in there.'

He thought we hadn't raised ourselves enough above the ground. The fact that we didn't have any time meant little to him. Rather than talk to me about his concerns, Ed's attitude was very much, 'I know what to do and I don't care that Ant is a survival expert: I'm going to do it my way.'

There's a difference between a boss and a leader. A leader will lead by example. They'll also be aware of and willing to expose their strengths and weaknesses because they know that the people in their team will complement them. Your weakness will be somebody else's strength. If I'd been the boss, I'd have forced Ed to conform. I could very easily have said to him, 'I'm the leader. No you're fucking *not* striking out by yourself. We're all cold, we're all wet, we need to sleep as one unit so that the body heat we're all giving off can keep us alive and let us sleep.'

My philosophy as a leader is to let enough rope out for people to trip up on. At the same time, you don't want to give them so much rope that they can hang themselves. In this instance, I wanted to let Ed learn from his mistakes. If he wants to do it his way, I thought, *let* him. He can't come to too much harm if things go wrong. Ed went off, waving his machete, obviously unbothered by the impression he was making. As he saw it, he was just obeying his survival instinct, and the rest of the contestants accepted his decision with good grace.

Ten minutes later, boom, it was pitch black. Ed was still building his own basha when it was dark. Fair play to him, he stuck to his guns and ended up sleeping on the jungle floor. That didn't make it any less funny the next morning when he woke up looking like the Elephant Man. He'd been dish of the day for the ants, mosquitos and a whole load of other jungle creatures. By the looks of him, they'd eaten well.

The following night there was none of the bravado he'd shown before, and Ed jumped straight in with us. It was still cold – I was tempted to use his long locks as a blanket – but I think we all got a better night's sleep. More than that, I could see that although his pride was dented, and he still wasn't quite in a place where he could accept his weaknesses or insecurities, he was obviously willing to learn. Ed was still a bit of a conundrum, but I couldn't wait to puzzle him out.

THE NEXT DAY we really got to work. After two or three hours of discussion, the engineers came up with a very interesting build. We'd create a boat from the roof of the bus, turning it upside down to form a makeshift hull. The idea was to use the engine from the motorbike as a form of propulsion.

It wasn't that straightforward, though. The roof wasn't going to just fall off the bus, so we needed heavy-duty tools to cut it off. And one thing I know about the jungle is that it doesn't have many branches of Screwfix. We had a guy called Chris, who was a maritime engineer. It felt as if this was a task that could have been designed for him, so I handed him the reins. This didn't go down well with Ed. He flounced off, flicking his hair and scratching his face.

With the tide coming in fast, Chris began delegating. He and I got to work with a hacksaw and crowbar on the roof of the bus, working furiously to try to salvage it before the whole thing got submerged. Elsewhere, the others were busy trying to scavenge parts from the old, decaying, flooded machinery. It could be dispiriting work, as they had to be prepared to spend hours ransacking a vehicle and find nothing. This would have been troubling enough at the best of times, but it was given a sharper edge by the knowledge that our days were cut short by the rising tide.

One, then two days passed. Everyone worked with the mud creeping up their legs, sucking at their feet, extinguishing their energy with every step. It was impossible to stay dry or clean. And at all times we'd hear the high-pitched calls of the monkeys and birds, strange rustlings in the vegetation around us, and crabs scuttling in and out of the thick brown slime. It was a grim, unsettling environment.

What reassured me was that the engineers were all so clever, able to look at problems in ways I could never even have begun to imagine. It was exciting to watch the way their minds worked. Except, inevitably, for Ed. While the rest of us worked hard to cooperate, he seemed absorbed in his own projects. He did what he wanted, how he wanted, and had little interest in anybody else or their ideas. Even when he was persuaded to join in with us, he'd maintain a critical running commentary of his own. Complaining and criticising, almost under his breath, but just loud enough for others to hear.

Looking back at the footage, it's astonishing how rare a sighting of Ed was during those first few days. As the other engineers bruised themselves tugging and pulling at wreckage in the hunt for useful tools, he was – well, I have no fucking idea where he was.

Still, everything was going well on the bus until on the third day Chris cut his finger right open. We were in a dirty, humid, dangerous environment without access to antibiotics or clean bandages, and he was severely dehydrated after three hard days in the jungle. The danger was that infection would take hold and spread, so I had to make the tough decision to get Chris out of there. Within minutes he went into shock. He was finished – and so would we be, unless we could pick things up quickly. We were already behind schedule, and he was the one who had the intricate plan in his head.

At this moment, Ed jumped to the front of my mind. I knew he was full of bright ideas and wanted to step up, so I called him over and handed him a bit more rope, reminding him as I did so about the importance of delegation. I regretted this within seconds when he told me to grab a saw and make another attempt on the roof of the bus. Thanks. For. That. Like a good boy, I hopped to it. What made me pause was that he said to the women, 'You wait here, and I'll sort this out.' I didn't say anything. 'Let the rope out,' I thought to myself. So I watched and waited to see what would happen next.

For a couple of days after Ed stepped into the breach, everything went fine. The others, determined to make the team work, responded well to him. They saw that he had a way of expressing the thoughts that had been building up inside him, waiting to burst out, for the last few days. Now he could share his knowledge. The others were relying on him, and he rose to that responsibility. It was his skill and persistence that got the bike engine up and running, a moment that sent waves of exhilaration around the whole team.

None of this, however, would count for anything if we couldn't connect it to the water pump that would provide the forward motion needed to drive our makeshift boat out of the jungle. We needed to find something that could be used as a driveshaft. This was easier said than done.

Ed had reserved this task for himself. He slopped about in the mud, wading from one derelict vehicle to the next, rejecting every piece of metal that did not exactly correspond to the ideal tool he had in his brain. His quest consumed him so totally that he appeared unaware of what anybody else was doing.

While he was engaged in his doomed search for perfection, I was grappling with the roof. I was so covered in mud, I looked like I was wearing a bodysuit made out of it. It crept into my boots, into every last crevice of my skin. All the muscles in my body were screaming with exhaustion and pain, and the bandana I'd wrapped around my head was soaked in sweat, which poured constantly into my eyes.

I could see how much the jungle had taken out of the others too, especially by the seventh and final day. Our bodies were worn down, depleted and hungry. We'd forgotten how to move without exaggerated effort, or what it's like to have an arm that wasn't covered in what felt like a thousand mosquito bites. Most of all, though, the jungle had invaded our minds. It came to seem like such an overwhelming force, we couldn't believe we'd ever escape from it. The jungle never stops, it never pauses for breath, it never lets up.

After I'd spent another two hours beating the shit out of the roof of the bus, and basically getting nowhere, I was absolutely knackered. I sat up there for a few moments, taking a break. Across from me on the other side of the bank I could see Ed by himself, dividing his time between flicking his hair and fiddling with a bit of metal. Again and again over the last days we'd told him that we were in the jungle, so let's just bastardise something. Why not just give something a go? It *might* work. Again and again he'd ignored us. He didn't understand that something was always going to be better than nothing. Especially now, when we were so close to failure. If we didn't get out today, that would be it. I wanted to fucking kill him. Sitting there on top of the bus watching him, I almost felt as if I was having a stroke. A couple of deep breaths later, I returned to my task.

Crunch, saw, scrape. Another two hours passed. I took a break and looked up. The women were struggling through slime, grappling with jagged metal. Ed was sitting *exactly* where he'd been when I last looked. It was obvious that he was so engrossed in his own activity that he wasn't able to see the bigger picture. He flicked his hair ... and that was it. I lost it. I leapt into the river and swam across to him. I didn't actually realise I could swim that fast – anger has its uses. As I swam, I tried to work out what to say – and how to say it. As always, I concluded, honesty was the best way to attack the situation.

Once I got back to the other bank I gathered the group together and took charge. 'Ed,' I said, 'you've spent all afternoon and you've still got no shaft here.' He tried to interrupt but I carried on. I told him that the tools had been right there all the time, but that when a weakness had presented itself six hours ago he'd refused to step back.

Ed needed to be more honest with himself. I said, 'Ed, if you'd told me two or three hours ago that you were struggling with the hunt for the prop shaft and that perhaps it was time to see if anybody else had an idea, maybe we'd have been in a better situation now. Instead we've wasted so much time, and we don't have time to waste. We can't get those hours back. I've got a funny feeling, Ed, that you don't know what you're doing. We need a Plan B. What can we put together?'

Immediately another contestant, Neera – who, although she did actually have lots of experience, was worried that the others would think she was young and naïve, and so had kept quiet up to that point – popped up with a clever idea. Neera had been a little genius. She knew that, as she put it, it wasn't about perfection anymore, it was about 'getting shit done'. Her solution was an ugly bastardised piece of metal, but it was good enough. I told Ed that I was going to relieve him of his responsibilities and that I wanted him to help Neera.

You could tell he was completely done. Demoralised. To the point where I had to pull him aside and tell him that we'd been staring failure in the face since the beginning. 'You can't think negatively. The only option is to think positively right up until the very end. Let's not get carried away with the destination. Ignore the possibility of failure. Just tackle the journey with positivity. We might get halfway through and the failure that's been hanging over us will start to look like success. The further along that route we get, the more likely it is we'll find a solution.' As he readily admitted, all he wanted at that moment was to dig a hole and climb into it. Take twenty, thirty minutes, I told him. Think about things, try being honest with yourself, and when you're ready come back into the fold.

The thing is that although I found his attitude immensely frustrating, I refused to hold that against him. It's so easy to meet negativity with negativity. It can feel like the default option, even if experience should have taught you that it's likely to cause friction. But I wanted to try to change his mindset, and I could only do that by showing him that there was another way. Stubborn people are like children: you can't *tell* them anything. What would telling him to fuck off have achieved?

It meant that I had to hide my reactions to him and almost force myself to kill his negativity with kindness. I saw the positivity within him. Once I'd spoken to him, I sort of left him to his own thoughts.

As soon as my back was turned, he flicked his hair and smirked. Then he announced that he felt as if everything was being blamed on him, and that he wished that he had 'another engineer who was the same as me or better than me', so that they could 'bounce ideas of each other, sit back, have a drink and solve it. I'm talking to my subconscious, trying to solve this at the moment, and I can't.'

With that, his voice cracking with emotion, he strode off to sit weeping on the trunk of a falling tree. He watched the women laughing and joking as they bodged together a solution. He looked utterly defeated.

That was the first chink. He knew that he couldn't do this by himself. What he wasn't willing to acknowledge was that his weaknesses might possibly be offset by others' strengths. He saw the existence of a flaw in his own abilities as a problem rather than an opportunity. I can understand why he grew so emotional. We were all tired and under pressure, and none of us had had anything near enough to eat.

As I trudged back to the bus, saw in hand, I felt a twinge of disappointment. I was worried I'd let Ed down. Had I given him too much rope? Had he hanged himself? Should I have reined him in a bit earlier? I began to feel as if I'd been an irresponsible leader. I knew as well as anyone that once one member of a team gets infected by another with a negative mindset, then they're in real trouble. Someone who's already convinced they've failed is lost to you, and they're about as useful as someone with an injury. I thought that my misjudgement had left our little band with only me and the three female engineers. Negative thoughts began to creep into my mind.

I remember sitting there, back up on the roof of the bus, thinking that not only had we lost Chris, but it seemed as if we might have lost Ed too. Once your mind goes, that's it, you're done. While the women were fitting the pieces of their improvised jigsaw together, I was really struggling. The bus of doom was resisting all my efforts, and the whole situation was looking unworkable. Even I was beginning to believe that we really were stuck. 'Fuck,' I said to myself, 'we're done here.'

Hard as it was, I knew I had to try to counter those negative thoughts and do what I could to engineer a solution. I threw myself into trying to saw the bus's roof off, even though, in my heart of hearts, I knew that it wasn't working.

It was at that precise moment that something amazing happened. I saw Ed swimming across the river to join me. Standing there, armpit-deep in the brackish brown water, I was honest with him once again. This time, I was laying my own weaknesses open to him. 'I really need your help with this, mate, I can't do it by myself. What do you reckon, Ed?' My weakness had presented itself, and he realised that now was the time for his strength to come in. He'd learned so much about himself in just a few days.

Guess what? He had a solution. He explained how we just needed to remove the inner skin – I hadn't even known there *was* an inner skin – then we could simply hacksaw it free in two-minute shifts.

I was out of options and almost at the end of my strength. 'Let's do it.'

Ed was infused with a new energy and confidence. He was pointing to the bus, explaining what needed to be done. In turn, the rest of the team picked up on this. The failure that we'd been so convinced of was now flipping into a success, and we were becoming ever more certain that we'd be getting out of there. Suddenly answers were presenting themselves to all those problems that had seemed insoluble. We got the bus upright.

You could still see the new life in Ed a little later on when he was helping drag the newly severed bus roof across the water. Everything he did was dynamic, his hair swinging round his head with the force of his movement. Ed had realised what an asset he was, and how much we needed him. It was the culmination of a process that had been unfolding slowly over the seven days: the team understanding that they needed each other. By the end, Ed was bringing solutions to problems, where, earlier, he had only been bringing problems to solutions. Instead of treating them like inferiors, he was communicating with the others as if they were his equals, explaining every idea or decision. Finally, we managed to build the boat and head out onto the water.

Ten minutes later, our makeshift craft sank to the bottom: the engine could never pump the water we needed. After seven days, we'd run out of food and water. We'd failed.

Well, yes, but it was only a failure in the most narrow of terms. We'd failed the task, but there were so many successes along the way. We'd all grown in our different ways. For instance, I came out of there having learned loads about engineering because of the experience of being with Ed and the women. They taught me a different way to approach and solve problems. And look how *far* we'd got. If I ever took on something similar, guess what? I wouldn't be starting from the beginning; I'd be way along the road already. You can't call that a failure.

I still feel proud when I look back on that time in the jungle. How courageous Ed was to have looked deep into himself and then, when we needed him most, to leap forward. That was the real Ed. That night, as we were on a boat being taken out of the jungle, Ed said to me, 'I've learned more about myself in the last seven days I've been here than I have in the whole time I've been on this planet.'

When you're honest with yourself – as Ed had started to be – you know who you truly are. You know your strengths and weaknesses. You're confident enough to ask other people for help because you know you can't do it all by yourself. When people ignore their insecurities or weaknesses and pretend they don't exist, they're building a cage for themselves. Positive leadership is not about telling people what to do, it's about offering them opportunities to learn and grow in a secure environment. You give them enough rope to trip up on, but not so much that they can hang themselves. They'll fall over, graze their knee and say, 'I won't do that again.' It's a process that builds resilience, confidence and self-awareness. Without it, they'll never know what they're capable of.

'DADDY, YOU ALWAYS catch me.'

I apply the same principles to raising my kids as to how I behaved with Ed during that episode of *Escape*. You want to give them the excitement and confidence that means they can go forward and try things. And when they fail, they'll just dust themselves off and go again. And again. And again. Learning all the way, without them even realising you're teaching them to live life in a positive manner.

When my daughter was three we'd just moved to a new house. One day I was getting the telescopic ladder ready to fix a swing to the top of a tall tree. My daughter saw me, came over and said, 'Daddy, Daddy, I want to climb the ladder.'

'Go on then,' I said, 'climb the ladder.'

She got two rungs up, then looked at me. 'Daddy, what if I fall off and hurt myself?'

'But what if you get up there and you *don't* hurt yourself. Who says you're going to hurt yourself?'

She took one look at me and then raced right to the highest rung. Three metres in a flash! When she got to the top I said, 'Let go and fall back. Daddy'll catch you.' Half a second later she launched herself into the air. She knew I would be there to catch her.

That evening, I thought about what had happened. If I'd lifted her to the top of the ladder myself, I guarantee she'd never have let go and allowed me to scoop her up. At the back of her mind there would have been all sorts of doubts. But climbing up by herself, having been asked, 'What if you don't hurt yourself?', she was infused with positivity.

It meant that she could put to one side all the negative things she'd have absorbed from pre-school, from other kids or parents. And it's changed her. I can see that she's more confident. Less afraid of failing. All it needed was one encounter. When she's around me she's fearless. She's not reckless – she's still asking questions and feeling out her boundaries – but she trusts the sense of positivity she gets from me; it infuses everything she does. Sometimes, when I walk past her and she's standing on the stairs, she'll shout, 'Daddy, Daddy, stop!' and like a little monkey she'll jump to me.

The next second, as I'm holding her in my arms, I'll say, 'Bloody hell, baby, how did you know I was going to catch you?'

And she'll say, 'Daddy, you always catch me.'

SHOW NOT TELL

It's my children and Emilie who give me purpose and inspire me. They're my fuel. Their existence motivates me to want to leave a legacy behind for them. I'm not talking about money or anything material; I want to leave them with an example of how to exist in the world – to show them what hard work can bring them. I also want to build them a platform so they can go out and succeed in the most positive way possible. The lessons I've learned are valuable and have come the hard way. I'm anxious to pass them on because I don't want them to have to start, like I did, from the bottom. At the same time, however, I know that I wouldn't be doing them any favours by handing them everything on a plate. I don't want to rob them of the satisfaction of seeing what *they* can achieve for themselves.

Nothing excites me as much as watching them pick up new interests and passions. Nothing pleases me as much as seeing them become brave kids who go unafraid into the world. I can't tell them how to be like this. It's not something I can achieve by lecturing them. Instead I try to demonstrate it to them through my actions. By showing them how I conduct myself every day, I know I'll be able to teach them something without them even realising it.

If you're trying to be the best version of yourself, people will see that and gain inspiration from it. It's contagious. For better or worse, parents are energy sources. Children don't really listen, not even when they're seventeen, eighteen. They don't take any notice of what we say. Kids learn by what they see. They absorb energy from their environments.

Were you to sit a ten-year-old down and gave him a big lecture about how to live his life, he'd remember maybe one or two words from it. But they're watching your every single move: whether it's the way you talk to your wife, the way you approach tasks or the way you lounge around on the couch. If a parent behaves in a negative way around their child, then, guess what, their child is going to grow up with a negative mindset.

This means that as parents we carry a huge responsibility on our shoulders. And yet how many of us can really say we're leading by example? I worry that we're becoming a nation of lazy parents. We're so concerned with ourselves, we're so narcissistic, that we forget that if we start acting like kids, our kids will start acting like babies. There's a knock-on effect.

Adults, increasingly, are acting like teenagers. Teenagers, more and more, are acting like children. Children are regressing into babies. There are adults who can barely look after themselves. They play the victim all the time and think only of me, me, me. Their kids don't stand a fucking chance. No wonder there's a whole generation of children who stick their heads in their laptops or tablets and never come out.

We're supposed to be taking steps forward in life, not tumbling back! I was so pleased when, recently, my daughter came up to me and said, 'Daddy, I just want you to know, I appreciate how hard you work. Everything we have, it's all through you and Mummy working hard.' I never mention how hard I work to my children. I've never sat them down and said, 'I slave all day so you can have a nice life, so don't mess up!' I wouldn't do that to them. But the fact that she wanted to share that thought with me shows that on some level she'd noticed.

That's not to say I'm perfect. Sometimes I have to catch myself. I'll be sitting down, watching the television, and I'll find myself, almost without really knowing I'm doing it, about to call out to my daughter to bring me a drink. The words will be in my mouth, and it's only then that I think about how lazy I'm being and what kind of an example it sets her. It's easy for me to go into the kitchen to get that glass of water, or to haul myself over to the sideboard to pick up my laptop. They're small things, but they're so, so important.

PASS ON YOUR FLAME

As a parent you're not helping your child if you lay out a whole prescribed future for them. You shouldn't say, 'You're going to be a lawyer,' or 'You're going to be a doctor.' You can't feed them a dream. You should be a compass, not a map. All you can do is kindle that flame inside them. In my case my flame is positivity, so I can pass that on to them and help them look at life in a positive light. They can then build on that. For others it might be self-belief or determination.

When I talk to my children, I ask them: 'What interests you? What gives you that fire?' If they say they don't know, that's fine. 'Let's help you find it,' I tell them. 'And do you know how we do it? Trial and error.' Once you find that flame inside you, you'll know that it's there, and all you'll need to do is nurture the flame.

When my boy tells me he wants to be an explorer, I could say, 'Look, son. I'm not sure that's much of a career. I don't even know that there's very much of the planet left to discover.' But I don't. I encourage him. I tell him that I've got friends in the mountaineering business and that when he's older he can talk to them. Because I can see that there's something in the idea of being an explorer that excites him. Sure, he might not be another Cortez, Livingstone or Marco Polo, but do you know what? That excitement about discovering, about seeing and learning new things, that's such a powerful flame to have burning within him.

Emilie

We've both changed a lot over the years we've been together. For instance, Anthony is much less likely to drop everything at six in the evening, go for a meal and return in the small hours. That spontaneity is still there, but he's found other ways of channeling it, ways that don't end up with a stinking hangover. But what hasn't changed for us, ever, is the importance of the family we've created together. It's what has always glued us together. We love our kids, and love being able to spend as much time with them as we possibly can.

Bringing them up the right way is extremely important to us. I want my kids to have success in their own right, independent of whatever Anthony does, and for them to understand the importance of work, not just living off Dad.

I think that setting a good example is the best way of making sure that happens. Anthony might be on television, but I don't want that to warp the way his kids see him. When he comes through the door, we treat him like a normal person. He's special in our eyes, but as a father and a husband, not a celebrity. Gabriel thinks that having a dad who used to jump out of helicopters and fire guns is ultra-cool. And Shyla couldn't care less. Her dad's her dad, and she's not bothered by the rest of it. Sometimes when *SAS: Who Dares Wins* is on TV, we will watch it. She might glance at the screen for a few seconds, then she'll go back to her phone, which to her is about ten million times more interesting.

Our philosophy is: we'd much prefer to have a house that looks like a bomb has hit it, but that's filled with four happy kids, than to have a tidy home and miserable children. Life's too short, isn't it? That's something that comes from Anthony – the free spirit in him. We want our kids to be spontaneous and energetic and fun, but also to be polite and respectful.

I guess that's the thing. You have to strike a balance that you're comfortable with. A good example is Anthony's ideas about giving the kids enough rope so that they trip over and learn a lesson, but not so much that they hang themselves. As a mum, I feel torn by it. On the one hand I can still remember being a child myself. I wanted to be independent and I wanted to be given the chance to get something wrong until I got it right. When people tried to show me how to do things, it sent me mad! On the other hand, you obviously want to protect them. Anthony had a couple of the older ones on quadbikes the other day, and I could barely watch. When I told him that even the thought of it was killing me, he pointed out that they have to learn how to treat things like that responsibly. That they've got to learn how to do stuff like that safely.

I couldn't bear it, but I let him take the lead, because

whatever my heart might be screaming at me, my head agrees with him. No matter how much you want to, you can't protect your children every single second of the day. They have to learn independence.

LESSONS

Leaders should also be teachers. Create a safe space in which those you're leading can fail, learn and pick themselves up again. Give them enough rope to let them feel free, but not so much that they hang themselves.

Expose your weaknesses as well as your strengths. Unless you're willing to do this, you can't make a positive contribution in a team environment. Recognise that you can't do everything yourself, and open yourself up to inspiration from those around you.

We've all got different flames. You can't tell your children what sort of flame they're going to carry through life, but you can help spark and then nurture the flame inside them.

Positive parenting isn't about telling your children what to do. It's about showing them. Kids don't listen to lectures, but if you set them a positive example by carrying yourself in the right way, treating others well and acting with integrity, they'll absorb those values almost without realising it. The same is true of leadership. Be a leader not a boss.

Kids should be kids and adults should be adults. Your job as a parent is to protect your child, not to be a child yourself.

CHAPTER 10

THE GARDEN OF EDEN

WHEN I WAS in the SBS I lived in the shadows. As far as the vast majority of the population was concerned, I barely existed at all.

My life is different now. I have a career that means I have to push myself forward and engage with the world in a completely different way. If I do well, everyone knows. If I fuck up, there's nowhere to hide. Even, it turns out, if I'm on the other side of the world.

A lot of people failed to strike the right tone when talking about the coronavirus. Unfortunately, I was one of them. I really got it wrong. I'd left for New Zealand to film a show out there three or four days before everything changed. When I was at the airport it didn't feel as if we were on the brink of such an extraordinary rearrangement of the way we live our lives. Fans were still coming up to me at the airport, hugging me and asking for selfies. There was no panic.

Then I landed in New Zealand, a country that seemed to be even less affected. I don't think they even had any cases at the time. Their shops and supermarkets were still full of people going about their daily business. Nobody there seemed too bothered.

I was a couple of days into the filming when things started to change; slowly at first, and then quite quickly. My social media timelines were full of stories of people beginning to retreat into their homes, seemingly too afraid to venture outside, while at the same time people were ransacking supermarket shelves. I saw photos of healthy, strong men driving out with car boots full of rice, pasta and toilet roll, while the old, the sick and the vulnerable were left to feed off scraps.

That sort of selfishness didn't sit right with me, and nor did the idea of hiding from the threat. And so I responded in the same way I would to any incident like that. I recorded a message saying that if you were fit and able you should carry on going about your business, keep the economy going, and, if you could, help those less fortunate than yourselves. It was the kind of tough-love message I've been putting out since day one.

To begin with, it seemed as if I'd hit the right note. One day passed, and then suddenly the number of cases in the UK began to mount at a terrifying rate. Then another day went by, and the government changed their initial strategy and ordered the country to begin social distancing. If before, it had been possible to still believe that the virus could still be contained, and that we weren't going to suffer as Italy already had, it was now clear that we were facing the kind of once-in-a-lifetime disaster that felt like the plot of a horror movie. It was not the world we were used to. Over the course of a handful of days my message was rendered grotesquely out of date. What I'd intended to be a boost to people's resilience had become bad, dangerous advice.

Even then, I think, I struggled with the idea that doing *nothing* was the best way of combatting arguably the biggest crisis our country had faced since May 1940. Do nothing? *Every* bone in my body, *every* blood cell pumping through my veins told me that you don't run from a threat. You tackle it head on, and the positives will follow. I can't ever think of an occasion when I've hidden from a challenge. Nor did I like the idea of self-isolation, which smelled to me too much of people looking after number one, not taking care of those around them. I found the whole concept so uncomfortable. Staying still while this invisible enemy rampaged through the country? It just didn't make sense.

I was on the other side of the world, in a country that was only just beginning to feel the effects of the pandemic. Britain's days were my nights; my days were its nights, so I wasn't seeing or hearing the same things as everyone here. I felt dislocated, so far away from my family and everyone I loved. So far away from the routine experiences of British people.

It was only slowly, as I got phone calls from back home, saw messages online and read more of the news, that I got my head round it. I realised that staying home wasn't selfish, it was a way of helping others stay safe, and that some of the information in my first video had the potential to do harm: the exact opposite of what I'd intended. I had to clarify my position as soon as I could. That's why I deleted the first video and recorded a new one.

I talk about integrity all the time, about keeping things black and white. That's why it was important to me that I put my hand up to admit, 'Yes, I got that wrong.' I didn't want to do that typical celebrity 'apology' video in which they look as if they've been held hostage by the Taliban, and try to worm their way out by making up excuses or claiming they'd been misunderstood. I also made sure I didn't dwell on it. Some of the sentiments in my video had turned out to be wrong, but everything I did, I did sincerely, for what I thought were the right reasons. I corrected any errors, so there was nothing to beat myself up about. All I could do is what I always try to do: ask myself what I could learn from this situation. Pluck a positive from a negative.

One of the things I discovered immediately was that you can't tackle everything with brawn and muscle alone. Sometimes it's best to step back, keep safe and reassess the situation. You can't always just charge in. The positive I've drawn from making that mistake was that it has broadened my thinking. It was also a reminder that I don't always get things right, that I've failed before and will keeping on failing until the day I die. The moment you stop telling yourself this is the moment you'll find yourself in trouble.

* * *

FOR A LONG time, it felt as if the whole world was in a negative bubble. It was a difficult new reality to adapt to.

The lockdown was a classic example of a scenario that's been forced on people – where you don't have much control, where you literally aren't allowed out of the house for more than an hour a day. I had to work really hard to make sure I didn't let it define me.

It would have been so tempting, so easy, to just sit at home and complain about the havoc it unleashed on my life; to complain about the restrictions, to complain that it's harder than it used to be to get a fucking flat white. And I know that some people would have gone further, falling into a victim mindset and coming out the other side of the crisis thinking they're owed something. It's a slippery slope.

The situation was overwhelming, that's undeniable, but it was still possible to find ways to make it work for you. I remember saying to myself, 'The virus has smashed a hole through life as we know it. There's no value in moaning about it. Instead, take a look around. What's been shaken loose? What new things can I learn? Think about your skill-set, your experience, your inclinations. How can you mould what's happening now to fit your priorities? Sure, there have been some really negative impacts, but what opportunities have opened up that you wouldn't have been able to access before?'

As always, I used positivity to help turn a negative situation into a positive one. As soon as I got home and the dust had settled, I was able look around me and start tallying up the positives.

I realised that I'd seen my family more in a few weeks than I could remember ever doing before. I'd moved into a new home a few months earlier, but until the lockdown really got going I didn't have a clue where half the things in it were or how they worked. Without quarantine, I'd never have got to grips with the house I'd worked so hard to buy.

More than anything, I felt like I'd been given the gift of time. I've been grafting non-stop since the age of sixteen. Over the last couple of years I've been doing eighty- and ninety-hour weeks, which have dragged me away from my family for five or more months a year. It took a pandemic to ensure that, after almost a quarter of a century of working my arse off, I could sit back and enjoy what I've earned.

I had some breathing space in which to stop, reflect and strategise. I wouldn't have given myself that opportunity if it hadn't been for the lockdown. The voice in my head telling me I've got to work all the time had been silenced.

This period of quiet enabled me to take stock of things and evaluate what was most important in my life. I found that I was reflecting more than I had in years. I got so excited by the way I started thinking. Beforehand, ideas would flash in and out of my mind; over the weeks I spent in quarantine, I actually had time to develop them. Some were good, some I'd rather forget as soon as possible. But the process of thinking and analysing was so exhilarating, and I came away with the seeds of projects that I know will be brilliant. 'You watch what happens when they let me loose,' I remember thinking, 'I'm going to go absolutely fucking *wild*.'

Looking beyond my own life, I find the sense of community that has returned to the country so inspiring and exciting. Suddenly, people are looking at their neighbours – whom for the last few years they've maybe only nodded to – and realising they can rely on them. How amazing that people are finding that when they need help others are willing to put themselves forward. Even more inspiring is the fact that people are rediscovering the pleasure that comes from altruism. You never get a sense that anyone is asking, 'What's in it for me?'

We've learned to appreciate, properly appreciate, the NHS, the emergency services, the police and the military. These four institutions are pillars of our society, and we need to fortify around that. Strip everything away, and we've realised what's most important in our country. Facts have replaced emotions and we've gone back to basics, having understood that for a while we got a bit too fucking clever and clouded things with a load of other stuff that seemed important for fifteen seconds, but which we can now see never meant *shit*. Do the basics to a consistently high standard. Nothing else matters.

We're all in the same boat, we're all afflicted by the same fears. Now more than at any other time is the moment to look over the fence and ask your neighbor for help, or offer it to them. Nobody's going to tell you to get lost. Whereas before the virus hit? They *might* have said hello back. In lots of ways I feel as if we've rediscovered something that was always in us, but that for one reason or another has lain dormant for years.

At the end of the day, if you scrape away all the bullshit, one thing remains true: we need each other.

THINKING ABOUT ALL of this takes me back to the filming of *Mutiny*. When we reached Vanuatu we were on the bones of our arses. Hungry, thirsty, tired, practically crawling up the island paradise's beaches. Just desperate, really. We were welcomed by the local tribe, and for the next couple of days we stayed with them. We hunted for pigs and were allowed to wander in what they called the Garden of Eden. It's hard to describe it – fruit and vegetables grew everywhere, in mind-blowing profusion. The idea was that you could pick what you wanted, as long as you planted a replacement. On our first visit, my arms were overflowing with the most amazing exotic fruits; I was like a walking greengrocer's.

As I made to leave, the tribe's chief came up to me and told me to put my basket down. We're going to another garden, he said. 'Fucking hell,' I thought to myself, 'more food!' The chief told me to collect the others, and off we went. I was expecting another garden filled with fruit. I thought maybe that this one would be even more spectacular than the first. Instead it was empty. 'What you've picked in that basket, you now have to plant twice in this garden,' he said. It took us four backbreaking hours. All we had was a stick to dig with, and very soon everyone's hands were covered in blisters.

The penny dropped. The chief was teaching us a lesson. Next time I went into the Garden of Eden I was far more circumspect; my basket was no more than a quarter full.

As we said our goodbyes the following day, I was almost over-effusive in thanking the chief. He'd been so generous and kind, far more than he needed to be. I remember shaking his hand as I told him how grateful we were, and that he continued to clasp mine even as I started to pull away. 'No. Thank *you*,' he said to me.

'But Chief, what are you thanking us for?' I asked. 'We've come onto your island and you've given us everything. It should be us thanking you.'

Still he gripped my hand. When I looked up into his eyes I could see that he was welling up. 'No, Anthony, thank you. Thank you so much.'

I couldn't understand. Again I asked him why he was thanking us when it was he and his people who'd looked after us. We were just guests who came with nothing and took everything.

'I wanted to thank you,' he explained, 'because you've restored our faith in mankind.'

'What?'

'You came to our island in your ragged boat. Tired, no food, nothing. See this island here? We have superyachts turn up filled with rich people who want to buy up *everything*, the whole island. This island isn't for sale. We always say no, no matter how much money they offer. And then you came along. You proved to us that if you take away every material possession, just as you have, then we're all humans, we're all the same and we all need each other. I'm sure you live lives full of plenty back home. Here, though, you came just as who you are. That's the biggest gift you could have given us.'

He thought that the world was lost to greed, selfishness and consumerism. Our tired, exhausted crew, stripped down to the essentials, had showed him that there were still green shoots of hope. I think we saw those same green shoots during the lockdown. It was the ultimate positive message. I hope that they survive.

WHAT DOESN'T KILL YOU

On a bleak, windy November day in 1997, a skinny kid with thick black eyebrows and the faintest hint of a French accent stepped nervously through the gates of Pirbright Camp. He was so thin that it looked like a strong gust of wind might knock him off his feet, he had the innocence that comes with growing up in small village in rural Normandy and he was unbelievably excited about what lay before him.

If only he'd fucking *known*.

Sometimes it can feel as if I've crammed more than one life into my first four decades on this planet. There are days when I find it hard to believe that I've seen and done so much. I've been a Para, a Marine, an SBS sniper, a policeman, a diamond trader, an author, a public speaker and a TV presenter. I've been up Mount Everest, into the darkest reaches of the jungles of Papua New Guinea, and I've escaped the horrors of an Ebola outbreak in Sierra Leone.

I've experienced the grief that almost exploded my existence twenty years after my father's death; I know the pure, unfettered exhilaration of combat; I've been crushed by the humiliation of waking up drunk and bruised in a police cell; and every day I feel the intense joy that accompanies watching five beautiful children grow and thrive.

Writing books has allowed me to share all of this with my readers. I see *Zero Negativity* as the final part of a trilogy that began with *First Man In* and continued with *The Fear Bubble*. In my first book I showed readers my life, in my second my soul. In this, my third book, I wanted to share as much as I could about how my mind works. Each of the volumes is a kind of waymarker, showing where my head was at that particular moment. Anyone who reads them will be able to trace the way my thinking has changed over that period. In that sense, they've also been a brilliant way of exploring who I am. I know that I'm a work in progress, and although I never want to get to the point where I feel as if that process has come to an end, I do feel like I'm getting closer.

This trilogy has given me the space to learn how to open up and be honest about my demons. There's nothing that makes you feel more vulnerable than having your weaknesses printed for thousands of people to see. But then there's probably nothing else that's so empowering, that makes you feel so free.

It was essential to me that my books should be as much a record of my mistakes and fuck-ups as they are a celebration of the things I've got right. I'm no more of an angel than you are. But I am somebody who's willing to admit that. Honesty is one of the most positive traits out there. It is to negativity what garlic and sunlight are to vampires. That's why I've never wanted to hold anything back. And that's why I've never wanted to shy away from taking my readers to places that might make them feel uncomfortable.

My life is an example of the way that getting things wrong is as natural as breathing. What I hope more than anything is that people come away from reading these pages with the understanding that, far from something to be afraid of, every mistake offers incredible opportunities for growth. You might feel like you've tripped up, but if you approach mistakes with a positive mindset, then you actually have the chance to take a huge leap forward.

I'd never pretend that acquiring a positive mindset is as simple as just snapping your fingers. I might be a naturally positive person, but I'm not sure I've always had a positive mindset. It's something I've built over time, the result both of all the experiences I've shared with you and also the concerted energy I've invested in training my brain. The message I spend so much of my life spreading these days is that there's nobody who can't do the same if they're willing to dedicate themselves to it. You can train your brain as easily as you can train any muscle in your body.

It's work that's more than worth the effort. The more you train yourself to think positively, the more you'll be able to smell negativity a mile off. You'll know, before it even comes into your life, whether it's the kind of negativity you can flip into a positive, or the kind that will drain you of energy and bring you down. I'm now in a position where I can use that good negativity as fuel to make me a better person. The bad negativity I can just bat away. Fuck off, I'm not even opening that door!

I can't tell you to follow in my footsteps. That desire to develop a positive mindset has to start with you. But if I can't make you set off on that journey, I can at least hand you a map to guide you. *First Man In, The Fear Bubble* and *Zero Negativity* are all part of that map.

* * *

IF WRITING THESE books has helped me make sense of my past and present, they've also given me an opportunity to try to begin to work out what my future might look like. That's why I feel that, although *Zero Negativity* marks the end of this trilogy, it also represents the beginning of something else. No matter how much life I've got behind me, I still don't feel as if I've got going yet; I still don't feel as if I've really *lived*. Turning forty holds no fear for me. The idea of the next decade excites me so much.

Even now, I don't know what I'm really capable of; I don't know what's waiting for me. At the moment I feel as if I'm pursuing the career I was born for, but that could change. Another route might open up. I don't limit myself.

That's why I feel excited when I wake up every morning. And that's why when I go to bed, I'm frustrated because there weren't enough hours in the day to wedge in everything I wanted to do. By the time I'm forty-five, I want to have businesses where I'm making money when I sleep. If I told you that in five years' time I'll be the multi-millionaire owner of one of the biggest tech companies in the world, you'd tell me to shut up. But then five years ago, when I was still in the military, if you'd told me that I'd be a TV star and bestselling author, I'd have told *you* to shut up. Nobody ever expected me to be so adaptable or versatile. I don't think many expected me to still be going. Fuck them. Luckily, I've always had faith in myself.

I know that as long as I'm always true to who I am inside, I'll be able to keep on taking bigger and bigger steps. The moment you conform to what other people expect you to be, you restrict yourself. If a business opportunity comes up, I'm not going to listen to the people who say, 'You're not a businessman, Ant. What *are* you doing?' If I'm interested and excited by it, I'll commit, then figure it out when I get there.

OCCASIONALLY I FIND myself wondering: what if someone had taken the naïve kid I was on that November day all those years ago to one side and told him what was coming down the road? Would he still have walked through that gate?

I always have the same answer: yes. Absolutely 100 per cent yes. In life, you have to commit to the unknown. If you're a positive person, you won't be afraid of what's round the corner because you know that you possess the tools to cope with whatever fate throws in your path. More than that, you know that you'll be able to turn those unexpected events to your advantage.

I know that when I get things right, I get them seriously right. When I get them wrong, I get them seriously wrong. I'm comfortable with that. I've overcome the death of my father, prison, the storms of Everest. I've even learned to overcome my own fears. So there's not much now that can knock me off my stride. I used to think that the saying 'What doesn't kill you, makes you stronger' was a bit of a tired old cliché. Now I understand how true it really is.

ACKNOWLEDGEMENTS

MY AMAZING WIFE and children whom I love so fiercely! Emilie, Oakley, Shyla, Gabriel, Priseïs and Bligh. You are my life.

To my brothers in arms: Damian O'Brien, Jez and Arf the twins, and Mike Morris. Your loyalty and commitment to better not only yourselves but others too, including myself, is unrivalled. Thank you!

To Josh, a great pleasure to have you so involved in my life, helping to make this book a true reflection of how I see the world. Not forgetting my friend and work-companion Jack Fogg. It's been a heck of a ride, mate. Thank you!